AMAZON ORDER: 106-6586645-0348248

Awakening *the* Brain

WATCH VIDEOS WHILE YOU READ

BEYOND WORDS AUTHORS ON YOUR SMARTPHONE

Tag images like the one above are placed throughout *Awakening the Brain* to bring you instant videos directly to your smartphone and enhance your *Awakening the Brain* experience.

To watch these videos, simply download the free
Microsoft Tag app at http://gettag.mobi.

Then hold your phone's camera a few inches away from the tag images,
and you'll immediately be brought to the videos
Charlotte Tomaino is referring to.

CLICK IT. READ IT.

Or you can visit the *Awakening the Brain* YouTube channel at
www.youtube.com/user/awakeningthebrain.

Awakening *the* Brain

The Neuropsychology of Grace

Charlotte A. Tomaino, PhD

ATRIA BOOKS
New York London Toronto Sydney New Delhi

BEYOND WORDS
Hillsboro, Oregon

ATRIA BOOKS
A Division of Simon & Schuster, Inc.
1230 Avenue of the Americas
New York, NY 10020

BEYOND WORDS
20827 N.W. Cornell Road, Suite 500
Hillsboro, Oregon 97124-9808
503-531-8700 / 503-531-8773 fax
www.beyondword.com

The information contained in this book is intended to be educational and not for diagnosis, prescription, or treatment of any health disorder whatsoever. This information should not replace consultation with a competent healthcare professional. The content of this book is intended to be used as an adjunct to a rational and responsible healthcare program prescribed by a professional healthcare practitioner. The author and publisher are in no way liable for any misuse of the material.

Managing editor: Lindsay S. Brown
Editor: Julie Steigerwaldt
Copyeditor: Sheila Ashdown
Proofreader: Jade Chan
Illustrations: Dennis Di Vincenzo
Design: Devon Smith
Composition: William H. Brunson Typography Services

First Atria Books/Beyond Words hardcover edition May 2012

ATRIA BOOKS and colophon are trademarks of Simon & Schuster, Inc.
Beyond Words Publishing is a division of Simon & Schuster, Inc.

For more information about special discounts for bulk purchases, please contact Simon & Schuster Special Sales at 1-866-506-1949 or business@simonandschuster.com.

The Simon & Schuster Speakers Bureau can bring authors to your live event. For more information or to book an event, contact the Simon & Schuster Speakers Bureau at 1-866-248-3049 or visit our website at www.simonspeakers.com.

Manufactured in the United States of America

10 9 8 7 6 5 4 3 2 1

Library of Congress Cataloging-in-Publication Data

Tomaino, Charlotte A.
    Awakening the brain : the neuropsychology of grace / Charlotte A. Tomaino.
      p.   cm.
    Includes bibliographical references.
    1. Brain. 2. Mind and body. 3. Self-actualization (Psychology) I. Title.
QP376.T633   2012
612.8'2—dc23

                                                2011053031

ISBN: 978-1-58270-311-4
ISBN: 978-1-4516-2827-4 (ebook)

The corporate mission of Beyond Words Publishing, Inc.: *Inspire to Integrity*

Contents

This book is dedicated to all who are seeking this information, including those who desire brain expansion due to injury or developmental limitations, those who seek spiritual expansion, and those who are aging and are approaching another life stage to be transformed.

Acknowledgments

Getting an author's inspiration onto paper and into your hands, eyes, or ears is a vast undertaking in our technological world, and I have great appreciation for all those who have contributed to and expanded my journey with *Awakening the Brain*.

First, my sincere thanks go to Mollie Rogers, Sister Janice McLaughlin, and all the Maryknoll Sisters, past, present, and future around the world. It is from you that many learn of the potential power of spirit and belief, what it is to be a woman living from belief for the betterment of others, and the strength of community to surpass our individual limits, especially back in the days when glass ceilings were everywhere and options were few. Your guidance has enabled me to live and now communicate this dimension of the inner and outer worlds.

Thank you to Grandmother Agnes, one of the Thirteen Grandmothers, for focusing us on the significance of always putting Spirit first in the Spirit-Mind-Body Connection.

Acknowledgments

Great appreciation for all those who have partnered with me in this creation. Sister Pat Murray, Mary-Ann Bunting, Dr. Jay Dunkle, Maria Martinez, Mimi Trotter, Sisters Consuela Torrecer, Rosemarie Milazzo (you started this), Rose Lauren Earl, Ann Hayden, Dolores Geier, Dolores Mitch, Rose Corde McCormick, Drs. Paula Grimaldi and Bruce Wilson, Barbara Zwick, Dennis DiVincenzo, Sue Palmer, and Sisters Helen Phillips, Theresa Kastner, Genie Lorio, Helen Werner, Pat Ryan, Maureen Gunning, Sandra Galazin, Lilla Hull, Phyllis O'Toolle, Rita Ann Forbes, Ann Maloney, Camilla Kennedy, and Cecelia Ruggerio.

To Cynthia Black and all my partners at Beyond Words and Simon & Schuster, thank you for all the ways you have improved on my expression of these concepts and taken them places where I did not even know to go. Special thanks to Julie Steigerwaldt, Lindsay Brown, Dan Frost, Tim Schroeder, Marsia Gunter, Georgie Lewis, and Devon Smith.

Finally, thank you to my family of origin and all those seeking this information, especially those who have come to NSW for assistance, AmmaBhagavan and those at the Oneness University, and Esther and Jerry Hicks. The questions you have asked and triggered in me have brought forth these concepts.

Introduction

Treating clients with brain dysfunction became a passion for me after my older sister suffered a brain injury that changed the course of life for my family and for me. The pain of this event was a driving force in my career; I moved from focusing on learning disabilities to developing my own model for treating brain trauma—one that could go beyond the limits we experienced in seeking care for my sister. Although it was my life's biggest unwanted challenge, this event has been my greatest source of growth and has enabled me to impart a perspective to others that I would not otherwise have to offer.

It is important to me that you know that everything in this book is real. All the neuropsychological brain functions and brain images explained here are the basis for the brain rehabilitation methods I use to assist patients in my office. All the stories of clients who have succeeded in achieving improvement in cognitive, emotional, and behavioral change are true events, although

I've changed the clients' names. The stories from my own life that I have included here were selected to convey specific real-life experiences of brain function that over time I have used to provide a sense of hope to the clients who seek this information. **The single most profound message that I have repeatedly received from those patients who have persisted in their recovery and achieved their goals is that if they were given the option of the brain injury, they would do it again because of all they'd learned and the ways they'd grown.**

At first this was hard to comprehend. The pain and struggle involved are not desirable. But slowly, my patients showed me the specific ways that, because of this intense journey, they had acquired the "pearl of great price" in what they each had achieved. Each person who has said this has reached a place in themselves that was not accessible to them and now is treasured. When you are in the midst of a huge challenge, expanding your abilities and letting go of the past, it isn't usually possible to confidently state that perspective. But many patients who have gone through this "dark night" have been transformed in the process. They have achieved health, skills, inner peace, awareness, and a lifestyle where they have found expansion. They have found their inner strength and clarity about what is really important to them in life.

I wrote this book because over the years many people facing brain-related challenges have asked me what they could read about expanding brain function. Some were interested in helping children succeed, while others were adults wanting to excel in their careers or enhance the course of their aging process. Some, like me, were related to someone with a brain injury and wanted to understand and help. Some of these people have wanted to grasp the power of spirituality as a source of strength in overwhelming times. Because I am a trained and credentialed neuropsychologist, a member of a family that faced these issues, and a former nun before all these events came to pass, I offer stories that combine information on both neuroplasticity (the adaptability of the brain) and spirituality. This is both an unusual and powerful combination to write about. It's the most powerful combination I have yet encountered. As the title of the book, *Awakening the Brain,* conveys, we have the potential to make neurochoices every day if we are aware and have the information on how to do it. By neurochoice, I mean a choice based on the intention to expand your neuropsychological ability. And this goes for healthy, well-functioning brains as well as those with limitations. Guidance from neuropsychology, combined with the power of belief in that which has not yet manifested, produces miracles that can become a "new normal" for ourselves and others.

The subtitle, *The Neuropsychology of Grace,* points to the second dimension of interest for me, which is belief and that spiritual power available to us, often called Grace. *Grace* is an ancient term used in numerous cultures and religious traditions. It's like the word *prayer*—easily understood but hard to define. As you will see, my interest is in sharing my observations on Grace and the neuropsychological principles involved in such human functions as intuition, synchronicity, and belief. My desire is for spirituality to be relevant to life events and for belief to make sense. This is the basis for combining science and spirituality in the stories and concepts offered here.

With all this in mind, this book is designed to provide information for your brain, hope for your heart, and inspiration for your spirit. In chapters 1, 2, and 3, my intention is to give you a perspective on this combination of the brain and its capacity to entertain a belief and live from it. Here I share with you concepts of brain characteristics, functions, and structures that combine to produce the change you desire. There are stories of awakening that come from history, like the power offered us by Buddha in achieving his enlightenment. There are stories of people like you and me who have also woken up to their potential and made their dreams become a reality.

In chapters 4 and 5 I focus on the current neuropsychological perspective about emotions and how they work in the nervous system, affecting you cognitively, physically, and behaviorally. My purpose here is to convey how emotions enhance or detract from both our effectiveness and our enjoyment of life. Managing emotion and using it as information about our circumstances, but not becoming the emotion we feel, is a crucial concept for making effective neurochoices. Being able to observe your emotions and shift them when needed changes your course. In chapter 6, I offer you the methods we use when doing neuropsychological rehabilitation treatment in my practice at Neuropsychological Services of Westchester in New York, with stories of the improvements people have achieved.

Chapters 7 and 8 are focused on how the brain, using thoughts in the frontal lobes along with executive functions, can be effec - tive in shifting emotion and sustaining belief. I also offer you a theory about how this happens, plus stories of extraordinary people I have known who have lived these principles and created realities from their visions. Here we look to people of faith, like my friends in the Maryknoll Missionary Sisters. There are lots of people overcoming challenges and offering inspiration to the world. How do their brains do it? This is a question worth considering. They have created meaning in the lives they live, no matter what the world is doing. In chapter 9 we explore further how the brain creates the meaning that sustains and enriches us, and look at some of those in our world who inspire us to do the same.

Finally, chapter 10 is specifically focused on three ways you can shift your own experience when you are not coming from the place in your self where you can achieve your intended result. I call these bridges, and they will get you from one internal state to a more desirable one. The first, the Freedom Bridge, offers methods that lead to immediate relief from an unwanted state. The second, the Joy Bridge, leads to your best and happiest self, no matter where you start. And the third bridge is the Expansion Bridge because when you are free and intend to be joyful as you take action, you expand into the future you desire. My goal with all this is to offer you a perspective that I have developed from having seen it and experienced it myself.

Interspersed throughout the chapters you will also find boxes in which I've explained some of the more scientific and historical aspects of the neuropsychological and spiritual topics we cover. I have also included Awakening Applications at the end of every chapter to guide you in incorporating these neuropsychological concepts into your daily life.

This book is all about how the brain awakens to belief. The single most important thing in your life is your awareness. What is in your awareness determines your experience of yourself and of your life. More specifically, this book is all about how your consciousness shapes your perception of events, which then determines your emotions and reactions to them. The perspective discussed here offers an awareness of the choices available to you and the brain mechanisms that facilitate these experiences. Once you are aware of the benefit of embracing and refining your beliefs and the power of your brain to create the outcome you seek, you can train your brain to orient to the events, thoughts, emotions, and choices that manifest your belief. I am beginning to think that this is what it means to use my whole brain instead of a localized function operating in isolation. I am beginning to realize that this is what great leaders, teachers, and sages have always done.

Although I was trained to write in neuropsychological terms to describe the brain functions produced by intertwined neurons, the facts in this book are presented in story form. The stories about the brain are designed to speak to your heart, your soul, and the right hemisphere of your brain through the language centers of your left hemisphere. You will better understand what that means when you read the book.

The world is entering an era in which the amount of information your brain receives exceeds its capacity to process in the traditional analytical way of the left hemisphere, creating brain freeze. We are evolving into an age where the right hemisphere, deeply connected to emotion and intuition in the body, will surpass the left hemisphere in effectiveness. We must learn to think globally and act locally with alignment to an intention, and if we come from the heart and our deepest level of awareness, we will expand our effectiveness for this new age of complexity and opportunity we are entering. There is a wordless well within each of us where embodiment of our deepest awareness, greatest strength, and most meaningful purpose awaits the words and actions we will use to create our reality.

Once you grasp some of the neuropsychological concepts, this book also points the way toward learning a new way of reading the information from your body. You already learned to read once, and now you are able to comprehend the symbols in this book to expand your concepts about yourself and your brain. This book is also about learning to read the other languages of the body and the brain. Each has its own alphabet and concepts. Just like we read body language in others to interpret and comprehend the meaning of their message in their tone of voice, facial features, body postures, and movements, there are body languages to comprehend the deeper meanings of our own experience. The languages I am referring to are the language of emotion and the message of guidance it contains; the language of body sensation, which I call the Brain-Body Compass, to guide us to our "true north"; the language of intuition; and the language of synchronistic events. As neuroscience studies the brain and reveals its complex functions, we get better insight into how to use all these sources of information if we can read the language it comes in.

Neuropsychology is the field that has identified, measured, and interpreted cognitive and behavioral functioning of the brain. Now my interest is in exploring the languages of emotion, sensation, intuition, and synchronicity. I offer these thoughts to you so that they brighten your journey over the Expansion Bridge to a fulfilling future. Once you awaken to your neurochoices and see the way your life changes when you regulate them and expand your brain, I am certain you will share the feeling of those I have treated: you will never want to return to your former way of living and experiencing the world. That is the "pearl" that awaits you too!

1

The Awakening Brain

What is an awakening brain? It is a concept that is at the heart of the approach I take in relating to the clients who come to me for information about their brains. The more awake you are to what is going on and to the possibilities of what could be, the more effective you become. The more information you can impart to others, the more aware they are of their choices. The more aware you are of the thoughts, emotions, sensations, and actions that are a part of your experience, the more awake and better able you are to choose your direction. It is as simple as that.

So what does "being awake" look like? Well, just as when we awaken from sleep in the morning and open our eyes to the physical world around us, our consciousness moves out of the reality of slumber and dreams. So, too, can the brain awaken from a level of consciousness. Each new day provides experiences that expand our consciousness if we allow ourselves to take in the awareness and realize the implications. As a child grows in experience, she learns to pick herself up after a fall, dust herself off, and pronounce herself to be OK. Once Mom has soothed the pain, slowed the tears, and returned her from the shock and fear, her own observing inner self can wake her from the same experience next time. In this way, she can move through the inner world of thought, emotion, and physical sensation to choose a better-feeling perspective.

This is the beginning of the brain awakening from the experience of the moment, recognizing and utilizing the power to choose the thoughts, emotions, and physical sensations that arise from within. Once Mom has said, "Nothing is broken, so let's go see what the dog is doing," you begin to learn how to awaken from your inner experiences and gradually are able to make that shift yourself.

There are endless versions of the "skinned knee" scenario throughout childhood. We've all experienced missing the most important party of the school year because of a family event, dealing with a pimple, or getting over being seen with a bad haircut. As adults we look back and chuckle at how our little worlds seemed to be coming to an end. The power of our disappointment, loss, and embarrassment was so great, but, with time, we have woken up to a bigger perspective on life; now those emotions, which consumed us at the time, have faded into a humorous story that yields the joy of being able to laugh at ourselves.

So what has happened in the brain since the days of those dramatic childhood events? New experiences connected new neurons, which began to talk to each other for the first time and produce a new awareness. When we awaken to a new awareness, the landscape of our lives expands, the possibilities grow, and new choices—never before observed and not even imagined—become very real and accessible. A new consciousness is awakened.

Awakening through Stories

As I mentioned in the introduction, the thoughts, experiences, and knowledge that I am sharing with you here are based on my life experience. As the result of a strong, early faith, knowledge acquired, and insights gained, I have woven together a perspective on both the inner world of thoughts, emotions, physical sensations, and knowing and the outer world of relationships, career, community, and service. As a neuropsychologist, I can unequivocally say that there are no two brains that are the same, and there never will be. Hence, my experience will not be yours. However, it is only experience that truly teaches. That is why much of the information in this book is conveyed in stories. As we experience our own reactions to stories, we discover our own truth. Other people's stories have shed light on the meaning of my journey, which is only mine to create, so I offer you my stories, which can open possibilities for you as you manifest the content of the days of your life.

Alice Walker perfectly conveyed this point about the power of storytelling:

> The process of the storytelling is itself a healing process, partly because you have someone there who is taking the time to tell you a story that has great meaning to them. They're taking the time to do this because your life could use some help, but they don't want to come over and just give advice. They want to give it to you in a form that

becomes inseparable from your whole self. That's what stories do. Stories differ from advice in that, once you get them, they become a fabric of your whole soul. That is why they heal you.[1]

It is my intention that your brain and consciousness will expand as you take in whatever here is uniquely intended for you.

Awakening the Brain is about experiences I have had and information I have learned from both my formal education and, more importantly, my education from the people I know who have transformed their brains and their lives. These are the insights and concepts I have become aware of because of my life experience. I am telling you these stories because you are reading this book to find greater insight and knowledge for growth and expansion in your life. We all learn from each other. It is my intention that you will learn from these stories and neuropsychological information and benefit in your way as I have benefited in mine. Our experiences and the awareness we glean from them are processed through that magnificent organ—the brain. The more you know about how it works, the more you can work with it.

Awakening the Brain Starts with Learning How the Brain Works

As a clinical neuropsychologist, I was trained in neuroanatomy and neurophysiology to understand the physiological processing of the brain and where its functions are located among the intricate wiring that weaves in and out of the folds of tissue in our heads. But more importantly, I was trained in standardized measures of cognitive abilities like memory, attention, language processing, and visual spatial processing to understand just what those neurons are doing for us. That means these mental functions can be measured and quantified to develop a picture of a person's cognitive talents or weaknesses and their level of ability compared to others who are the same age.

THE FIELD OF NEUROPSYCHOLOGY

The field of neuropsychology is a division of psychology specializing in brain function and how behavior, skills, and experience relate to the brain structures and their processing of information. Brain function is evaluated by objectively measuring cognitive skills like attention, memory, or language with standardized tests, and comparing skills of those the same age. The pattern of strengths and weaknesses in an assessment is used to educate, advise, and treat functional challenges and achieve desired goals.

Neuropsychological evaluations serve a variety of purposes. For example, when a person considering a career change or an educational opportunity seeks guidance about their likelihood of success, a neuropsychological evaluation can reflect a view of his or her "peaks" of cognitive strengths and "valleys" of limitation, showing where the person may not be competitive in the desired setting. From that perspective, we can analyze the demands of the education or career being considered in light of the person's present cognitive strengths or weaknesses. This provides a fairly solid basis for making a big, life-altering decision and helps a person invest in those efforts that have a greater likelihood of success.

The more aware we are of what we are working with, the better our insight and judgment for the decisions we make.

Within each of the brain's primary cognitive functions lies the subtler underpinning for processing that information. Language, of course, is divided into our ability to express thoughts as well as our capacity to receive spoken language and comprehend what is being said. Within each of those functions, there are numerous finer skills, like vocabulary, use of complex sentence structure, ease of accessing words, speed of processing, melodic intonation in speech, and precision of articulation.

CONSCIOUS COGNITIVE FUNCTIONS OF THE BRAIN AND SENSORY PROCESSING

Sound: Expressive and Receptive Language
Vision: Perception, Spatial Relations
Motor: Coordination of Movement
Smell, Taste, Touch
Proprioception: Muscle Information
Attention: Focused, Alternating, Divided
Executive Functions: Organization, Planning, Anticipation, etc.

Memory has turned out to be especially complex, with many different types of memory and characteristics in its use. We have memory for what we see, hear, taste, smell, and identify through touch. There is the immediate memory for information you are working with as you read this book as well as short-term and long-term retention of the information for future use. But that is just the beginning. What about incidental memory for the trivia that just stays with you, or procedural memory for driving the car, using the computer, or getting money from the ATM? Then there is the process of using your memory: how you take in information (encoding), how you hold on to it (storage), and how you get it back out (retrieval). We've only just begun to define and measure what goes on in the brain, and clinical neuropsychology is the discipline creating the tools and making them available when you need them.

The field of neuropsychology explores, defines, quantifies, and measures the mechanisms beneath the tip of the iceberg of language, memory, and all the other cognitive abilities the brain processes. The study only really started in the 1970s, and we're just now beginning to understand the potential applications of neuropsychological information. Still, at times this information reaches the general public. In 1994 I had a client who was concerned about difficulty focusing. She came in for a neuropsychological evaluation to better understand her abilities and limitations. After completing the evaluation and hearing about her cognitive style, she asked if I would provide an interview for her friend who was writing an article on attention deficit disorder, which was little known and less understood than it is today. I agreed, since the frontal lobe functions controlling attention had been a dimension of my dissertation research in the 1980s, and I had been teaching this material in educational settings. After doing the interview, I quickly forgot about it until a 1994 issue of *Time* magazine—its cover article based on that interview—hit the stands and my phone started ringing day and night. America had finally discovered the frontal lobes of the brain, and hundreds of people were learning that they were not crazy, stupid, or lazy—they just could not control their focus, and they wanted to do something about it.

During subsequent years, a broader, richer, and more helpful understanding of these cognitive functions of attention has revealed that there are many kinds of attention, such as the ability to first focus and then sustain attention on the topic without distraction. Then there is the ability to alternate the focus to something else and return to the original train of thought. Dividing your attention between more than one thing at the same time is yet another type of attention. Finally, silent concentration is a unique state often understood in a spiritual context. Each of these has a specific function and effect on all the other abilities in the brain. And that is only the beginning of exploring the amazing talents of the frontal lobes of the brain.

The field of neuropsychology has developed methods to measure all these unique and distinct conscious cognitive functions of the brain, map out where these functions are processed in the brain (called localization), and identify tasks that can strengthen them, if you want to. The more we know about how the brain works, the more we can do to get it to work the way we want. These are the concepts that allow us to observe ourselves, make choices from among our experiences, and be aware of what we are doing.

What is an awakened brain once we have grown up and have the ability to observe ourselves? Being awake begins with the awareness that all of life is an inside job. Neuropsychology teaches us that our thoughts create our reality. Once this truth becomes a lens through which you see the world, you become awake to what you are doing with your life. When you realize that the story you play in your head, both about yourself and other people, shapes your experience, and that you get to change or make up that story, you are able to observe yourself and choose the life you want. Anything you experience presents a choice for you to act on, or not. The story you tell about yourself is what you have chosen to become. A sum total of these stories and choices becomes your life.

How many times have you taken on others' opinions and interpretations but didn't feel good about it? This book offers you the opportunity to be aware that you have awareness and know that it is there for you to observe how you feel and choose among those paths in life that manifest your potential.

The Story of Awakening to Enlightenment

Back in high school in the early 1960s, I realized that I actually had choices that would shape my experience of life. I enjoyed reading, and one day I came across the book *Siddhartha* by Hermann Hesse, which is the story of a young man named Siddhartha who lived in the time when Buddha achieved his enlightenment. In the story, Siddhartha explores life and achieves much success in terms of knowledge, wealth, and social esteem. But he never finds the fulfillment he seeks. Something is always missing until, like Buddha, he lets go of his attachment to the material world and achieves his own enlightenment.[2]

Only many years later did I learn about Buddha's young life. At that time I did not know about Buddha. I had never heard of Buddhism and knew nothing of the teachings. But I loved the story of young Siddhartha's explorations and personal transformation. Somehow he was real to me. Hermann Hesse had captured the awakening process in the inner world through his story of Siddhartha, which paralleled the awakening of Buddha.

Buddha, prior to his enlightenment, was also named Siddhartha. He was a young man born to nobility who gave up everything when he discovered the suffering that existed in the world outside his father's palace. He had a passion to find the path for overcoming suffering and showed us that it is all an inside job. The story of Buddha's life, like the story of Jesus and many others, has succeeded in relieving suffering in the world by teaching an awareness of the elusive inner world that runs our thoughts, hearts, bodies, and actions.

After finishing the book, I sat and thought about this story of an awakening, sorting out the essence of the message and wondering what life would be like if I, too, could learn to do what Siddhartha did. Could I learn to fast, think, and wait? That was the message I got. The possibility of no longer being driven by my body's desire for food, no longer believing every thought and emotion I experienced, and no longer being controlled by my impulses was beyond my imagination but somehow seemed both desirable and possible.

The story of Siddhartha was not my story, but nonetheless it made real to me the potential in my inner world. The awareness that came from that story enabled me to notice my bodily sensations rather than be them, take my thoughts and emotions less seriously, and consider my options instead of reacting. The book awakened my brain to a way of living that was desirable for me and significantly influenced my subsequent choices in things I talked about, books I read, and interests in which I invested time and energy. Looking back on the experience, I am glad I did not know who Buddha was. Siddhartha was a young person I could identify with. He was real to me, which made that story inspiring enough to change my awareness and then change my life.

The awakened brain knows that I am here to open to the inspirations that come to me and, by reflecting on this collection of inspirations, gain insight that reveals to me what I need to know. My consciousness grows with each inspiration of my own and each revelation received from others, until I shape the concepts that are the basis for the story of my life. This is the path of my growth and evolution. I get to choose what I will do with the conscious awareness that I have developed. What I decide will determine my experience of life, my contribution in this world, and the legacy I leave to others.

Awakened Thinking

Awakened thinking is not for everyone. This type of thinking is for those drawn to and comfortable in the realm of belief. In this realm, awareness of the awakened brain is the platform of power upon which to create a life that is just the way you want it to be. This is not to suggest that the unwanted will not be there. It is simply your choice to decide where you are putting your attention and what you want to include in your experience. Any thought or emotion can be a source of focus to dwell on, like a conflict, or you can move on to focus on something more desirable, like a solution. Desirable emotions can be the resonance with the world that brings you satisfaction, or undesirable emotions can be the impetus to find satisfaction. Those thoughts that you decide to embrace are likewise shaped by the values and intentions with which you live your life. There are times when a rainy day is a welcome sight or a huge disappointment. Your experience of life is determined by the context of your thoughts and emotions, which shape your perception. The more awake you are to what factors underlie your perception of a rainy day from one time to the next, the more you are in charge of your life. The more you know your capacity and the options you have to work with, the more you recognize new options for your choices.

This is where belief comes in. A belief is a thought you have chosen to resonate with in order to grasp the meaning of your experience, because, right now, that is how you interpret your world. The Dalai Lama has told neuroscientists that he wants to know about their discoveries on the mechanisms of brain function; if they discover anything that convinces him that his beliefs are incorrect, he will pursue changing the belief. That is our evolution in process. The world was thought to be flat and then round. The universe was thought to be finite and now we are told it is on a continuous path of endless expansion. These scientific discoveries change the way we look at life, the way we think about ourselves and each other, and the deep-seated expectations we have for our future that does not yet exist. It is from the beliefs that come from our awareness that our world is created. It is from the thoughts we keep thinking that we see and actualize the possibilities into realities, or not.

All this is based on my choice to expect with certainty that which has not yet manifested. When I align with an intention from an inner KNOWING that the outcome is assured, I am always able to think from that expectation and sustain my effort to completion. No one in my biological family had ever achieved higher education, yet the field of neuropsychology so fascinated me that I decided to become a doctor and somehow believed that I could become one. Lots of people have no experience in their life of a physical reality that suggests something is possible, but somehow they do it anyway. When you consistently focus on your belief, you prime your brain to expect and see the steps necessary for the outcome you seek. But without a belief in a possibility, you will not recognize outcomes that are there, waiting and available to you. Each choice you make is based on an expectation of an outcome. It's all about belief, every day. Your beliefs create what you see and expect, and hence they create your life.

The Power of Belief

Beliefs work for us and they work against us. They shape what the brain sees. One of my favorite examples of how powerfully our beliefs affect the processing of information is the example of the lost pen. All of us have experienced some version of this. If we look for the pen in the spot where we last recall seeing or using it and it is not there, the brain begins moving in the direction of recognizing "the pen is lost." Continuing the fruitless search further reinforces the brain's concept that, indeed, it is gone. That thinking alone is a belief that influences your brain to expect that you will not find the pen.

Depending on the significance of the lost pen, the brain can get us worked up into a real tizzy of frustration and a cascade of thoughts that can take over and send the subsequent day's events on a downward spiral. In our inner world, we can live out the consequences of the possible loss, long in advance of any actual event happening. What we expect can also blind us to what is actually there. Because the brain is focused on the story of the lost pen, it loses focus on what is actually in front of us. Hopefully, that magic moment comes along when some person who does not know the pen is lost simply points to where it is resting among the papers on the desk and everyone bursts out in laughter and relief.

Psychological research and daily life have shown over and over that this lens of expectation primes the brain. No two people walking down the same street at the same time are having the same experience. One is saying, "What a beautiful, bright, cool, crisp day it is. Look at the beauty of the fall colors in the trees!" The other can be saying, "Winter is coming, the light is fading, and the leaves are falling. I dread this time of year." Both are walking down the same street, living from the beliefs that color their perceptions.

How Experience Determines the Character of a Memory

Because of my first career as a nun, I have been blessed with an ongoing relationship over the years with the amazing women who stayed in the Maryknoll Missionary Community and have shared their expanding consciousness with me. They are my spiritual family, and I love sharing my inspiring stories of knowing them. What I have experienced and learned from my friends at Maryknoll has contributed to the perspective from which I see the world.

MARYKNOLL

The Maryknoll Sisters Community was founded in 1912 by Mollie Rogers, a Smith College graduate. By collaborating with the Maryknoll fathers and establishing this community, she created the opportunity for American women to embark on cross-cultural missions to offer service to the poor, with a focus on women's needs, and to "extend the Kingdom of God."

Maryknoll sisters do missionary work in Asia, Africa, South America, Central America, the Pacific Islands, regions of the United States, and Europe. They are primarily active in missionary services and also have a Contemplative Community in the United States and overseas. An affiliate program allows women and men who share the missionary charism (a unique spirit based on the founder's original intention and the spiritual path originally developed in the community) to be formally associated with the wider Maryknoll movement. The Full Circle Organization comprises members who were once in the Maryknoll Community, have since left, and maintain an active relationship with the sisters.

There are also communities of Maryknoll fathers, brothers, and lay missioners working in foreign countries.

In that family I have been a postulant, novice, doctor, friend, student, and teacher. I am a member of the Full Circle Organization, which unites all of us who have left the community over the years, and I return annually to the Motherhouse in New York for a reunion. Over the years I have been trained in the old traditions; I have been a friend to many, a student of the wisdom keepers, and teacher to some. Although I have done lots of teaching about the brain at professional conferences and during my years on the board of directors of the Brain Injury Association of New York State, my favorite audience is the nuns. There I am challenged by the questions and intrigued by the applications because their stories include experiences in countries, cultures, discoveries, and struggles from all over the planet. They have lived a life based on belief and have brought loving service in education, health-care, village cooperatives, women's solidarity, children's safety, and the preservation of elders' wisdom. They ask really unusual questions and apply the brain concepts that I teach from a unique perspective.

One such memory that comes to mind happened on a retreat I was leading for them. When the sisters return to the United States after years of foreign service, they come home to a program called "renewal," where a variety of opportunities are available for visiting family and friends, caring for their physical health, education, rest, and rejuvenation. In recent years I have been blessed to have the opportunity to teach about the brain and belief on their retreat. Many of the sisters work in very rural villages in Africa, the Islands of the Pacific, South American rain forests, mountain villages in Asia, or inner cities in Central America. Most have not had contact with evolving Western knowledge during their years in mission and have a lot of catching up to do.

On one such retreat I was teaching about the brain and emotion, specifically focusing on the potential of the brain for increasing wisdom during the aging process. We were doing a guided imagery meditation to work through the symptoms of anxiety, sleeplessness, and depression related to past traumatic experiences. Many of these sisters had worked in countries experiencing significant civil unrest and violent overthrows of governments. The contemplative communities in Guatemala and in the Sudan have brought a prayerful presence to regions in turmoil. Their presence in El Salvador came into international view in 1980 when two of their sisters died in the conflict. They serve the poor and live from belief.

MARYKNOLLERS
The Maryknoll Contemplative Community was established by the foundress in 1932, with the intention that the Community

be "a visible witness to keep alive the ideal and idea that every Maryknoll sister is a contemplative" in action. The stated purpose: "Our particular expression of mission is the ministry of prayer and sacrifice for all Maryknollers, the peoples they serve and the mission endeavor of the church throughout the world. . . .We forego an active ministry: believing that prayer in itself is profoundly apostolic." Since its founding, the Contemplative Community has had a presence in Ossining, New York City, New Mexico, the Sudan, Guatemala, and Thailand.

At this particular retreat, a large number of women in their seventies and eighties were home from foreign lands for renewal once again, but this time they were not going back. They had reached an age or level of physical health that indicated that the time had come for retirement from their life's work. Their week together on retreat was a time to tell the important stories of their lives. They came from all parts of the world, many not having seen each other in decades. Hence, this conversation was different from past retreats. It was about staying home this time. It was about finalizing a life's work as a teacher, doctor, administrator, or social worker in another language and culture where they had lived all their adult life but would not return.

This was a huge life adjustment. Retirement is big for all of us, but to leave your work, community, culture, language, friends, and favorite places is a lot all at once. What we think are problems here in the Western world are luxuries in the communities where people spend their lives traveling rivers in tropical forests and sleeping in hammocks to stay away from the creatures of the night. On this particular day, we gathered for a discussion about the earlier guided-imagery meditation, in which we had addressed disruptive and disturbing emotions.

The sisters shared their various insights regarding the memories and emotions of past experiences that continued to be triggered in the present. After a pause in the conversation, a soft voice entered the flow of sharing. The sister explained how she had enjoyed hearing about the brain and the chemistry of emotional experience. She had not known how it worked and did not identify herself as one who suffered from any kind of trauma. Consequently, she had thought the retreat was very interesting and appreciated the knowledge but did not see how it was relevant to her. Finally, while exploring her own inner world in the guided-imagery meditation, she began to notice memories that contained strong emotion. She was one of the group members who had come home to stay, and with that perspective she began to observe and reflect on the life she had been living for many years.

She had never suffered from the panic attacks, depression, or sleeplessness that had been discussed. She grounded herself in prayer and meditation practices daily and engaged in a spiritual community and her work as a teacher, all of which, moment to moment, had sustained her over the years. But in the guided-imagery meditation, memories returned to her. She paused in her comments, and we waited as she considered what she was hearing herself say and what it meant. Finally she said that at first it did not seem that any of this would apply to her. But now that she was considering it all, she realized she had lived under martial law for forty years.

There was a silence in the room as we all considered what she was saying. I thought about all the WWII veterans who participated in D-day, survived, came home, and stayed busy with family and careers for all those subsequent years. But when the fiftieth anniversary came around, hundreds of them came forward seeking assistance with nightmares, repetitive disturbing thoughts, disruptive emotions, and horrifying memories they could no longer ignore. The brain can file it all away until some event, association, or opportunity opens the file of that experience to be relived again.

As we continued in the sharing of insights, I encouraged each of the sisters to consider her power to choose her focus, observe her emotions, honor the scars she lives with, and respect the wisdom contained in her suffering. It is often our pain that causes us to reach for relief and grow in consciousness as a result. In response to the sister who shared her story of living for forty years under a military threat, I encouraged all of them to observe their thoughts, honor the memory of their emotions, and respect the rhythm of their bodies. I advised them against taking on diagnostic labels as an identity, which is a common suffering in the Western world. Those experiences are not who you are but rather information to consider. So much of our life experience depends on where we are coming from within ourselves at the time of the experience. That significantly determines the character of the experience and memory we take away with us. The nuns know there is a life force that keeps these brains and bodies going. They have an ancient language to discuss it and ways to access its power to sustain their efforts. When they can stay grounded in that awareness, martial law is not even on the radar screen.

Expansion through the Power of Belief

When we look at neuroscience's current focus on human brain potential, we see studies of the brains of nuns and monks who have spent countless hours returning their focus to a spiritual consciousness. In the '60s, I spent three years in "formation" at Maryknoll, which was spiritual training in the novitiate. These years were largely silent, for the purpose of growing in awareness of the inner spiritual realm and focusing on the theology and scriptures of Christianity. Developing a strong core of belief and purpose is the basis for an inner alignment that guides one's actions. It is developing an inner muscle that is stronger than the emotional and cognitive impact of the outer world. In those silent years of inner growth, I had experiences for which there was no language. To this day I can return to them in an instant as a source of grounding by realizing and integrating the complexity of my experience in the present moment.

The lives of the sisters on the retreat were different from mine in many ways, but there were lots of similarities. I did not live under martial law, but I did live in the inner city of St. Louis, Missouri, in the summer of 1967 while Detroit was burning down. I did work in cancer research for the Visiting Nurses of South Bronx, New York, interviewing women following their mastectomies, and I have spent thirty years journeying with people who suffer with brain dysfunction and injury. I have had my own fears, losses, and confusions, and have had to reach for inner spiritual stability while my brain and emotions sorted out what to do. From my perspective, there are seven billion unique versions of those dynamics going on around this planet, with all of us playing our unique part in this complex world we are creating together. The greater our consciousness of how the brain works, what the emotions mean, how to manage the body, and what the likely outcomes of our actions are, the more deliberately we will create the world we want.

Our thoughts, emotions, and behaviors are influenced when we live from inspiring and fulfilling beliefs. When you see the face of the Dalai Lama, you see the twinkle in his eye and the giggle bursting forth. How could this man be happy despite the destruction of his country and suffering of his people? When I consider that question, I also recall that joy is considered the infallible sign of the presence of God. Again, I am reminded that our life experience depends on where we are coming from within ourselves at the time. We form our own intentions and choose our focus. The Dalai Lama lives in alignment with the inner peace that he teaches is possible for all of us. **When I see his smile, I sense that if he can do it, I can do it. Each of us can make the choice moment by moment.**

What are the secrets of human experience that can help us understand these seeming contradictions? How can a glimpse into the brains of such people contribute to our growing understanding of the great human potential their lives reveal to us? These are some of the questions I explore from the perspective of understanding the neurological structures involved in the experiences, as well as the thoughts and beliefs that make them real despite the lack of physical evidence. I have learned that we all create the collective reality of the world, as we each make up our own collective reality. To grasp what that means, I seek to understand the inner-world mechanisms going on inside each of us that produce great and satisfying expansion, changing who we can become, like the effect of the vision that broke the four-minute mile. My career has enabled me to see such powerful creation come from normal people and has let me know we all have that potential within us.

Through the power of belief, we have expanded beyond what was thought to be the limit of the human capacity. For many years it was thought that men could not run a full mile in less than four minutes. Many tried in the 1940s and early 1950s, but none were able to break the record. Finally, three thousand spectators gathered at Oxford University on May 6, 1954, to witness Roger Bannister run the mile in 3 minutes, 59.4 seconds. The world record had not been broken for nine years, and it was commonly believed it never would be broken. To this day, Bannister's race is considered one of the greatest moments in sports. Since that breakthrough, numerous runners have surpassed that limitation as well. History contains lots of examples of limiting beliefs that have held us back, only to have one hopeful believer come forward to open the door to what is possible for many.

Recognizing Opportunity

Although I have reflected on thoughts such as the power of belief and expansion of human capacity for most of my life, their simple clarity comes and goes for me. The true gift is the deep, inner certainty of KNOWING that when clarity is gone, I can get it back. By sharing what I have learned about how my habits of thought shape my emotional state and color my perceptions and how I work with them, it is my hope that you, too, will be able to awaken to your thought habits and know that clarity is always within reach. A good example of a return to clarity happened to me when I decided to write this book. On a train ride from Seattle to Portland, I sat, looking out the window, wondering why I was going there. Having just returned from a truly uplifting vacation in Alaska, which had been a dream of mine for twenty years, my mind was resonating with the unfathomable beauty of the nature I had enjoyed upon finally seeing icebergs and whales in the wild.

As I looked out the window, my mind searched for the focus that had brought me there, traveling to a meeting with the staff of Beyond Words Publishing to explore the possibility of writing this book. But what was that intriguing focus that now was over-shadowed by a great vacation? What were the reasons I was so enthusiastic about going to Portland?

With these thoughts in mind, I entered the dining car of the train to have lunch and sat across from Kathy, a woman close to my age and also traveling alone. We chatted about what had brought us there and where we were going. She had just finished a road trip up the West Coast with her daughter and grandchildren and was returning to Southern California. She described herself as being in a major life transition. The children were grown, the marriage was over, the house was emptied of its memories and sold. She was in her own little home with her cat, her yoga, her freedom, and her opportunity to discover what was next. She was exhausted. Riding the train and looking out at the passing terrain brought rest and relief from the responsibilities of the past. The future remained unknown.

Her story prompted me to talk of a similar turning point in my life, after my mother made her transition. With the stress of my work treating brain trauma, my family's years of struggle with my older sister's brain injury, and my mother's transition following pancreatic cancer, I was left in a similar place where most of the lights had gone out. My health had suffered and I was exhausted, but I was also free of huge family responsibilities. As I shared my story with Kathy, I told her that one of the most impor-tant concepts guiding me at that time was my awareness of a scientific fact that the body replaces every cell it has over a seven-year period. That knowledge gave me a focus. In 2003 I gave myself seven years to engage in exploring the benefits of acupuncture, yoga, jin shin do, chi studies, massage, meditation, exercise, nutrition, hydration, herbs, supplements, reflexology, essential oils, and any other wellness-promoting practice that crossed my path.

Kathy asked me how I was doing, since it was now 2010 and my seven years were done. I told her that I was enjoying my full-time neuropsychology practice treating brain dysfunction and my part-time teaching about the brain, and that I was now on my way to Portland to talk about writing this book. All my former health limitations were gone. As I explained my own years of rejuvenation, I saw the light return to Kathy's eyes. They widened in an energized, interested, expectant way. She asked again if all my health challenges were gone and, when I again confirmed that to be true, she said, "That was what I needed to know."

It was visible from her facial expression that the thought of giving herself seven years to focus on and promote her well-being had connected the dots in her brain. She asked many questions about my work; the contents of this book; how the brain works; the alignment of focus, spirit, body, and action; and the benefits of physical health. An ease slowly came over her as we ate our salads, talked, and looked out the window at the passing countryside. When we were finished eating, she looked around the dining car and said, "The car is full but no one has come to join us at this booth. That never happens." She had been riding the train a lot when she traveled, enjoying the freedom from her memories of her past life that often replayed in her mind, because there she could focus on the world going by.

We agreed that we had met for a reason. I thanked her for the gift of this encounter, which was the answer to the questions I had held in my mind all morning. When I saw the way the dots connected for

Kathy and the light that went on in her eyes, I knew why I was going to Portland. Writing this book was all about my wanting to participate in the great shift in consciousness going on right now. Neuroscience provides knowledge and insight into our brain functions and our ability to achieve the growth and expansion that is possible. Being aware of how my brain works gives me concepts for choices in how I want to manage my own experience. I am not my physical health or state of my body. I am not my emotions or my thoughts. I am not bound by my relationships or responsibilities, though they have influenced me greatly. The life force that is me is free to choose among those influences setting a standard to live by and a vision to achieve. Having the consciousness to know this has transformed my life, and it has the potential to change yours.

Kathy departed the dining car while I waited to pay my bill. The last thing she said to me was that she wanted to dance the tango again. When I asked her why that appealed to her, she said she had always loved the tango for its complexity. Each partner actually moves with different steps of his or her own, which requires the dancers to be grounded in their own unique process, yet moving in perfect rhythmic alignment with the other. What a great metaphor for life. What a great place to come from within yourself as you approach your day. Kathy, if you are reading this book, please know that your contribution is appreciated. Let me know how you are doing with the tango of life. I got to reinvent myself. I hope you did too.

Synchronicity Is Happening All the Time

Over the years I have often wondered just how synchronistic events, like my meeting Kathy, happen. How does the right person come along at just the right time to create just the right outcome, especially when there is no way you could execute such an event even if you thought of it and tried to make it happen? Some events are clearly happening due to a causal relationship. I bought a ticket for the train, got on it, and got myself to Portland, Oregon. This is conscious cause and effect. But events like meeting Kathy while walking into the dining car and being seated with her by the train conductor cannot be understood in a causal context. However, it can be perfectly understood under a context of focusing the brain on patterns of meaning, a topic we will explore in more depth in later chapters. When we think in terms of the meaning as an organizing principle for that which we seek, we often find what we are looking for right under our noses. When I expect to find an answer to a question I am formulating, I examine my circumstances for the answer and along it comes. Sometimes the answer is found by encountering someone like Kathy or in a book or a random thought that lights up for me in that unique way. If I expect it to be there, it comes. Your expectation shapes your perception.

The idea of synchronicity is a concept that has to do with the relationship between ideas that manifest in life as simultaneous occurrences that are meaningfully related, not causally related. This is a fascinating area of study first developed by the psychol - ogist Carl Jung as part of his thinking about the collective unconscious, and influenced by concepts from physics and quantum mechanics through his conversations with Albert Einstein and Wolfgang Pauli. Coincidental events happen all the time but are often dismissed. The coincidental, synchronistic universe is there all the time if the brain expects to notice the pattern of events and relate to them as meaningful. What you want to believe and focus on is up to you.

Some people interpret synchronistic events as coincidence, answers to prayer, or signs of guidance. These are common comments we hear every day. For some with beliefs from religious traditions, such events are the result of Grace, for which I offer you my definition:

Grace
Gift of enabling power
Sufficient for progression
Conveyed by the Divine
To and through humanity

This definition is based on the belief that there is a power in the universe and you can access it when you reach the state within yourself that allows for receipt of the gift. When I talk about where you come from within yourself and the state you choose to act from, I am pointing to an openness to the resources or Grace that is available when you have a certain, positive expectation. We will be discussing this inner world and current theories about it in more detail in chapters 7 to 9.

Creating Your Own Wellness

When I observed Kathy's reaction to our conversation, I was reminded of my own connect-the-dots experience. I had a big realization when first struggling with my own stress-related health symptoms. This was the beginning of my awareness that my choices could affect my health. After graduate school in the 1980s, I had decided to go into private practice treating developmental brain challenges and helping patients recover from brain injuries. Although I was trained in both diagnostic testing and treatment methods at the best facilities available in the New York area, neuropsychology was in its infancy, having only been founded in the 1970s. Commonly, my day ended with a feeling of wishing I knew more or wishing I could seek the advice of other professionals experienced in these skills.

As it was, I was the only neuropsychologist in the area and daily had to explain to other healthcare professionals about the potential for recovery and growth in brain function that was coming forward from my discipline. Gradually, my infrequent migraine headaches became a weekly occurrence. Exercise and careful diet helped, but as the problem increased, I sought assistance from a local neurologist. After a brief exam and review of my symptoms, he recommended a new migraine medication that had just come on the market. He explained that he had been working on the clinical trials developing the drug and proudly assured me of the substantial pain relief they had measured in the studies.

Feeling reassured by his attentiveness, caring, and enthusiasm, I took the samples he offered, agreed to try them with the next migraine, and made my next appointment. Unfortunately, the next migraine headache came, but the medication did not produce the level of relief reported by others. In fact, it made me feel worse. After a couple of unsuccessful attempts, I returned to the neurologist. Upon hearing about my lack of success, he attempted to convince me that it really would work. He believed in his research on the drug and sincerely wanted to help me. But when he offered more samples, I knew this was not the way.

Reflecting on this impasse between us, I casually asked, "Do people who have migraines like mine ever have them stop?" In his fervor to further convince me to take the samples, he said, "Of the people who have your profile of migraine symptoms, **only 11 percent ever get free of pain**." This response obviously contained his argument for taking the samples and trying again. However, in my mind, new dots connected with that statement. What I heard him say was, "Of the people who have your profile of migraine symptoms, only **11 percent** ever **get free** of pain."

After a moment of reflecting on the possibilities, I asked if he knew how the 11 percent did it. Since he had just completed extensive research at the medical center on this topic, he was quite knowledgeable and told me of all the alternative therapies, lifestyle changes, and health-promoting practices that were known to be helpful. In that moment I decided to join the 11 percent who had succeeded in becoming "pain free." I told him of my decision, thanked him for the guidance, and left, never to return. If it was possible for them, it was possible for me! That was a major step in the beginning of my active interest in learning how to create my own wellness. It was a moment of awakening to my ability.

Inventing or reinventing yourself by knowing how your brain, emotions, thoughts, body, and intentions work together to manifest the life you want is the potential of the awakening brain and the story this book is offering you. There are countless stories like these—some in your own life, I am sure. It is the power of your choice to focus on what you desire that will determine what you see as a possibility for you and what you act on to create your life.

If you decide to continue reading from this point on because you want the benefit of understanding your brain and beliefs, open your mind to the possibility of becoming what you are learning here. All of life is made through dreams that come alive because someone believed in them. Don't waste your time reading more if you are going to argue with the offerings, resist their contribution, or attempt to find evidence to refute them. Belief is not arguable. Focus on what is true for you, not what is true for someone else. This is a book for people of belief who want to know how their brain manifests their intentions and who want to create their life more consciously and precisely. A common concept in our society is the Mind-Body Connection, which can worry you to death or enhance your well-being. This book is about the Spirit-Mind-Body Connection and explores the dimension within us that can observe the mind as the brain is chattering away. By being able to observe the mind, you can learn to manage your brain to enhance and create your life as you want it to be.

Awakening Applications

◆ The brain awakens when it recognizes and uses the power to choose the thoughts, emotions, and physical sensations that arise from within.

◆ When we awaken to a new awareness, the landscape of our lives expands, the possibilities grow, and new choices become real and accessible.

◆ Once you are aware of the power of your brain to create the outcome you seek, you can train your brain to orient to the events, thoughts, emotions, and choices that manifest your belief.

◆ A belief is what you have chosen to expect with certainty, even though it has not yet manifested. When you align with that belief, you are able to think from that expectation and sustain your effort to completion. Try this in your own life; it is as simple as picking something to believe in, believing in it, and then observing the results. Record your thoughts and observations in a journal; that way you will begin to see how choosing your beliefs, which are the platform for the consciousness through which you see the world, directs your decisions and actions.

◆ You hold the power to choose your focus. Focusing on what you desire will determine the actions that create your life. Start today: In your journal, write down a Goal Statement containing the Objective you desire, the Action required, and the optimal Timeframe. Then spell out an Action Plan with the specific steps necessary to get there. In my practice, patients are the most successful in manifesting their desires when they commit them to paper. See for yourself.

Notes

1. Cathryn Wellner, "Storytelling Is a Healing Process," Story Route, http://storyroute.com/2010/05/14/storytelling-is-a-healing-process/ (accessed 11/13/11).

2. Hermann Hesse, *Siddhartha* (New York: New Directions, 1951).

2

The Brain and Change:
By Choice or By Chance

Time often seems to stand still, and usually we experience ourselves as being the same today as we were yesterday. As many have said before, all this is an illusion. The earth continues to rotate around the sun whether we are aware of it or not. Likewise, the billions of neurons and the trillions of connections between them in each of our brains keep changing with every experience, even when we sleep. We are in a state of constant change that *can* happen by choice or *will* happen by chance. We are evolving in every moment with the chemistry of each sound, sight, thought, and emotion that passes through the brain. Thanks to neuroscience, we have a new consciousness about our inner dynamics. And as you begin to understand your dynamic nature and the movement of chemistry that never ceases, you glimpse the importance of being conscious and making choices. **Change is inevitable. The only question is whether you are going to have something to say about it**.

Charlotte A. Tomaino, PhD

A Crash Course in Neuropsychology

To understand how you can influence change through choice, some neuropsychological basics will be helpful. Even though we don't see them in action, our conscious mental experience is facili‑tated through tiny cells called neurons. Understanding how our neurons work enables us to enhance our experience in a variety of ways. Each neuron conducts an electrical charge called an action potential. When that charge fires, chemistry is released from one neuron and taken up by another. Just as electrical impulses flow through electrical wires to convey information, they flow through our neurons to convey information. When billions of the neurons in your head release chemistry into trillions of those connections, you come alive.

Action Potential: Video of a neuron exploding in the energy of an action potential and conveying its message to the neuron receiving the message across the synaptic cleft, the space in which neurons meet and communicate.
http://www.youtube.com/watch?v=iUnH1f2-pks

Neural networks are an important concept to grasp if you want to get a glimpse of your complexity. The billions of neu‑rons in your brain talk to each other, and the more they talk, the more likely they will be to talk again. This is referred to as neuro‑plasticity. When we take the time to reflect on our experience and see beyond the surface events and the old automatic reac‑tions that have driven us, we are literally connecting new dots in our brain.

NEUROPLASTICITY

Neuroplasticity is a physiological ability in the nervous system, referring to its capacity to adapt and change. When new neurons connect, you have a new experience, and that is how you can develop new skills. A physical change occurs in the nervous system when you experience change in thought, emotion, or behavior. Changes occur on all physical levels from the very small cellular level to the large level of neural networks that interconnect functional locations in the brain. The word *plasticity* is used because your experience is literally shaping the structures of the neurons in your brain. The brain is like a muscle; the pathways processing your experience get stronger the more they are repeatedly activated. The word *entrain* means to engage specific neurons and then train them in a function. Neuroplasticity enables you to change your mind and view the world differently based on new experiences that connect neurons in your brain in a new way and entrain new skills.

Each choice we make creates a focus for the brain and guides neurons to talk to each other, creating new connections or reinforcing old ones. When we realize that someone's criticism of us comes from that person's own fear or insecurity, and we actually make the choice to feel some compassion for those who have hurt us—a daily spiritual practice for nuns and monks— we have connected the dots of insight and perspective for a greater objectivity the next time something like that happens. If we keep thinking such thoughts, we actually reduce our own suffering by cultivating different emotional reactions that will then automatically come from life's events.

Automaticity is the characteristic we strive for when attempting to master a new skill. The nervous system is highly adaptable, hence the plastic component in neuroplasticity. It is the repetition of a thought or action that eventually makes it automatic. When learning to read, we first had to sound out the letters. But slowly, automaticity kicked in and the automatic recognition of the word made reading become fluent. Automaticity happens with anything we keep doing. With repetition, we shape who we become.

The reverse is also true. Skills and insights that are no longer reinforced with experience will decrease with time and may become lost. We can also foster negative behavior. If we reach for a drink, criticize someone else, or act out of frustration, the likelihood of that behavior growing to be automatic increases. Repetition of our behaviors strengthens their likelihood of becoming automatic. Neuroplasticity has an upside, where it improves skills, awareness, and quality of life, but it can have a downside, where painful and destructive behaviors take over and keep getting stronger, imprisoning us in bad habits. Every thought, emotion, and act leaves a trail of neurological footprints within you. These are traces of your experiences that neuroplasticity can either build or diminish based on your choices.

In my work I use a video depicting two neurons that have never communicated actually moving toward each other; the dendritic branches of the neurons reach out and attach to each other to convey a chemical message. When I show the video to patients to explain their potential for recovery, a look of hope deepens in their faces. It all becomes more real and very possible. When I show it to audiences at conferences, they want to see it again and again. When people actually understand that the choices of what they focus on are shaping their brain, a new level of awareness is available to them. Focused choices of thought or sloppy thinking have implications for training your brain. The video depicts what is happening in your brain right now as you connect new dots with a new awareness that is awakening you to how your brain works.

 Neuroplasticity: Two neurons that have never communicated reaching out and attaching to each other to convey a chemical message. http://www.youtube.com/watch?v=FWr6DXDhQx8

When you are building new neural networks as you first learn a new skill, you are selectively engaging a specific set of neurons, teaching them to work together to automatically go into action when you have mastered the task. When you first get behind the wheel of a car, you start the transformative process in your brain that will, over time, take your identity from being a passenger to becoming a driver. When you change your neural network, you create a new dimension of yourself. When children are small, we read to them. As they mature and master the skills of literacy, they become readers. When you can read or drive, whole new worlds open up to you. You train your brain to become the person you are. These are fascinating concepts with enormous potential for awakening in us a consciousness of who we are and the potential for what we can become. In an existing network of neurons already talking to each other, new connections can be made and contribute to the existing network.

Neural Network: Existing network of neurons talking to each other and new connections being made and adding to the existing network. http://www.youtube.com/watch?v=UtkN5wF9RB4

A relatively new perspective coming from neuroscience imaging of neural networks now suggests that there is a progression of change in the pattern of neural networks that unfolds with age.[1] As data on the areas of the brain that automatically talk to each other in young children were compared with the networks talking to each other in adolescents and adults, significant differences were observed. In children, the brain regions forming networks were physically close to each other and based on local proximity in the brain. Neurons nearby found each other and established communication to facilitate basic functions of walking, talking, and eating. The language center for storing words finds the neurons that control the mouth muscles, and out come the words. They are physically located adjacent to each other in the left frontal lobe. But as our experience broadens, our neurons reach out to distant locations in the brain.

The interconnections keep changing as we grow. In adolescents, and even more so in adults, the neural networks link neurons that are distant from each other but functionally related. For instance, the visual center sends messages to the neurons for the letters of the alphabet and then on to the thumbs to move across the BlackBerry. The neuroscience imaging shows us that, over time, repetitive events activate a connection on a functional level to produce the automatic response desired. With time and repetition, your thumbs automatically go to the keys your mind imagines.

A key principle of neuroplasticity and neural networks is represented here. As the Canadian psychologist Donald Hebb put it, "The neurons that fire together wire together."[2] Repetitive thoughts, emotions, and behavior increase the likelihood of strengthening that experience to become automatic. This is a good thing when it comes to learning to drive a car and not wasting time to think about putting your foot on the brake when a child is chasing a ball into the street, but not so good in the case of destructive reactions to stress that become addictions.

The neural networks you build and continue to reinforce will become the automatic reaction you have and will eventually help you become who you are. Knowing you are a work in progress is the power of the awakened brain. We have all seen and heard of experiences that seemed impossible. Spontaneous remissions from disease, breaking the powerlessness of addictions, forgiving the unforgivable and achieving a joyous heart, and going to foreign lands to serve the "untouchables"—all are in the realm of the impossible for many who have never seen otherwise or who feel powerless to think any other way. However, if you explore these extraordinary events, you find ordinary people who changed their thinking and took a leap of faith, believing in what others thought impossible. Why is that? Somehow the vision and expectation held in their mind, along with the physical and emotional state of knowing it to be possible for them, created the outcome they sought. Their inner reality was greater than the outer reality they had known and, hence, enabled them to do the seemingly "impossible."

This is neuroplasticity at work, guided by your desire and inspiration. When the brain is focused on an intention that has emotional meaning and drive behind it, your inner physical resources are marshaled to adapt and engage neural structures that have not previously talked to each other. Repetitive effort increases the automaticity of any behavior. That is how the nervous system works.

A Story of the Brain's Awe-Inspiring Ability to Change

With an awakened brain, you have the potential to train your own brain to achieve experiences you desire. But this is not an uncommon experience; it is happening all the time. Let's consider a common case in point. Children with specific cognitive abilities and weaknesses are born daily. Dyslexia, or an impaired ability to read, is a commonly known cognitive style that creates challenges in school. Similarly, some children have difficulty comprehending and using language, visual, or motor skills. Early intervention with physical, speech, or occupational therapies identifies the basis for the developmental challenge and engages the child in tasks that will strengthen those abilities. This is an example of the potential of neuroplasticity, engaging the neurons of the brain to talk to each other and expand their functional ability.

A striking example of the power of neuroplasticity to expand functional skill can be seen in the outcome for a child that came to my office a number of years ago. Barbara was a very special little girl. Her parents brought her to see me because they were concerned about the results of the intelligence test administered in school. They were educated people, committed to their children, and curious about the brain. Barbara was obviously smart, but the IQ test showed her to be in the average range, consistent with 50 percent of children her age. Her parents knew that Barbara was not average. She had talents and she had challenges.

She was born prematurely and had been receiving therapies for delayed development in motor skills, including speech articulation, since she was three years old. Barbara's parents knew about neuropsychology and wanted to know more about her development and what would assist her growth.

On review of her IQ test results as a nine-year-old, it was obvious that Barbara was not an average child. The overall Full Scale IQ score on the Wechsler Intelligence Scale for Children is an average of many subtests measuring those verbal and visual skills considered to be the most important for successful cognitive processing. Lots of people want to know what their IQ is, but since the Full Scale IQ is actually an average of multiple subtests and composite scores, it is possible to tease out the underlying skill levels contained there.

CALCULATING INTELLIGENCE QUOTIENT SCORES

The Wechsler Intelligence Scales, which measure IQ, contain four composite scores that are calculated from multiple subtests. The cognitive functions now considered to measure intelligence include verbal and visual skills, working memory capacity, and processing speed. When extremes in ability are averaged to obtain a composite score, unique patterns of processing information can be obscured.

Embedded within the "average IQ score" was a measure of extraordinary verbal talent. Barbara had a verbal IQ up at the 99th percentile, which is only seen in 1 percent of our population. Now, that is extraordinary talent. The problem was actually found in her

Visual IQ score, which was down in the 13th percentile. Combining her two IQ scores at the top and bottom of the scale results in an average overall IQ score that obscures the real picture of what is happening in those cortical hemispheres, the part of the brain where our skills for conscious functions are located. This was a child with brilliant verbal skill, but although her eyes were perceiving what was before her, the visual information from her eyes was primarily not available to her brain for use in her functioning.

Her parents discussed how Barbara was doing at school and at home. Her father expressed his concern that on a bike ride down the block to the corner store, Barbara could not find her way home. They knew she was struggling and often anxious in situations in which she felt lost. Her mother talked about how Barbara stayed close to them, never venturing too far. What was obvious to others was not obvious to Barbara, what with the limited visual information available to her. Separation anxiety had been something I had consistently observed in children with these visual or spatial processing limitations in the evaluations I had done over the years. This sense of confidence in finding one's own way in the world is grounded in an internal map to which information is being added daily. Barbara's map was largely not available to her. Her brain was not connecting the neurons that would help her make sense of the world visually. After some additional testing of Barbara's visual system, it was more obvious which skills were not spontaneously developing and instead required training for her to achieve the independence her parents envisioned for her.

Since neuropsychology is the field that also retrains the brain after an injury, and because this service is also offered in our office, we had lots of tasks for Barbara to do to make the information perceived by her eyes available to her brain, hands, and body. Her parents were highly committed to making this developmental opportunity available to her. Even though there were lots of breaks in the remedial sessions for play dates, school activities, and vacations, Barbara persisted in training her brain to use the information her eyes had to offer. She got better at finding her way home as well as seeing what was going on in science and geometry. After two years of visual and spatial processing exercises and visual motor tasks, Barbara graduated from her remediation sessions and stopped seeing me because she was now more independent.

COGNITIVE REMEDIATION FOR DEVELOPMENTAL CHALLENGES
Cognitive remediation refers to treatment intervention tasks that strengthen brain function in conscious cognitive abilities such as reading, attention, visual processing, and language skills, and usually focuses on academic skills.

COGNITIVE REHABILITATION FOR BRAIN INJURIES
Cognitive rehabilitation refers to treatment intervention tasks that retrain the brain's cognitive functions that have been impaired by injury. When the neuropsychological evaluation can identify areas of impairment, these skills can be retrained.

Then, four years after their first visit, Barbara's parents returned, seeking more information to enhance her success in the challenges of middle school. Barbara, now thirteen years old, came in for testing again, once more producing an average Full Scale IQ score. Her extraordinary verbal talent remained in the 97th percentile. However, this time her visual IQ was at the 45th percentile, a 32-percentage-point increase in her intelligence score measuring her brain's ability to use visual information, two years after stopping her remedial skill training.

It was a happy day when I saw that! In graduate school I had been taught that IQ does not change. But here was Barbara, four years later, with a huge increase in her visual intelligence. That is the power of neuroplasticity if you know how to use it to work for you! When you purposefully know how to use neuroplasticity, you can change your brain to increase your ability. Now, this might sound like the climax of the story but it's not. Six years later, Barbara's parents called again to arrange another reevaluation so that her accommodations for extended time would continue in college.

Rarely do we get to observe the adult level of skill for kids we have worked with in a clinical setting. Barbara came to the office the summer before her sophomore year in college to do the neuro-psychological evaluation again, and we were able to arrange for her extended time on tests to continue through the rest of her college education. More importantly, for my curiosity, the testing provided a measure of how her visual skills were now developing as an adult. To everyone's delight, her verbal IQ remained in the very superior range in the 99th percentile. Her visual IQ, however, continued to rise and now was in the 73th percentile, 60th percentage points higher than the original testing.

Barbara's test results represent an important point about cognitive style. When we look at the combination of all the cognitive, emotional, and social skills a person has developed, we can talk about the cognitive style with which they view and function in the world. The word *style* refers to the unique ways we function. Certain characteristics give music a "classical" style, writing a "stream

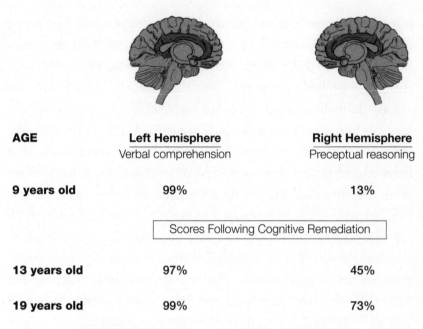

AGE	Left Hemisphere Verbal comprehension	Right Hemisphere Preceptual reasoning
9 years old	99%	13%
	Scores Following Cognitive Remediation	
13 years old	97%	45%
19 years old	99%	73%

Figure 2.1 Barbara's neuropsychological evaluation results

of consciousness" style, or architecture a "modern" style. Our brains have a style too. Sometimes a person's cognitive style is characterized by a strong and precise vocabulary, natural mechanical ability, outstanding athletic skills, or quick wit. These styles are all grounded in an underlying brain organization they have been born with or that they have developed. Your cognitive style also influences your spiritual perceptions, beliefs, and the meaning you create, all of which will be discussed in later chapters.

Barbara's cognitive style is best characterized by outstanding verbal skills. Her vocabulary is as good as it gets, and her fund of knowledge is vast. She is an avid reader and recalls what she reads. She can think abstractly and explain what she knows. Her verbal abilities are natural and extensive. Just don't ask her to put together the new toys for the cousins' birthdays when they arrive unassembled. The visual, spatial, and mechanical skills are something she has to think about, plan out, and put effort into. Although she has improved enormously over the years, her visual skills are not as automatic and natural as her verbal skills. The peaks and valleys of her cognitive style have remained the same, but the reduction in the extremes have made them manageable and reduced her anxiety. Her awareness of what she needs to do when tasks require visual processing allows her to compensate for that original style if she is motivated to stop and think about it. With visual tasks, she must take extra time and make a deliberate effort, which she does not have to do with verbal material. By being awakened to her cognitive style, Barbara became was aware of her natural talents, her challenges, and the options available to her. (If you are interested in a neuropsychological evaluation to determine your own cognitive style, you can find a list of recommended doctors on my website, awakeningthebrain.com.)

MULTIPLE INTELLIGENCES

Intelligence was originally considered a unitary concept. It was considered a single mental function, and people had varying degrees of ability. You were smart or not. Gradually, as the brain was better understood, it became clear that the brain does many things, all of which are a part of intelligence. The ability to acquire knowledge is different than the ability to figure out novel circumstances. Visual intelligence is different than verbal intelligence. Academic skills are only a small part of the abilities we need to succeed in life. Social, emotional, musical, mechanical, mathematical, linguistic, and athletic skills and spiritual awareness are all natural talents that people are born with as well as ones they develop. Hence, the concept of there being many forms of intelligence is far more helpful than just an IQ score.

As Barbara's test results came in, an additional finding was emerging. It is commonly the case that once more severe limitations in the brain's ability to process information are treated, difficulty can be observed and addressed in the underlying finer skills in that sensory modality. For instance, if a person is highly distractible, it is not possible to know the extent of skills like memory that are so affected by attentional fluctuations.

On this evaluation, we discovered that Barbara was having trouble recognizing and remembering faces, which is a discrete function of the visual system. In severe cases, this challenge is diagnosed as prosopagnosia, or face blindness, and can be the result of injury to the brain as well as a developmental challenge. When people like Barbara are not aware of a limitation like this, they become anxious in situations that require the skill and often shy away from such settings because they are not enjoyable. For Barbara, the facial recognition difficulty now requires that she develop a skill where she pays close attention to people's facial features and pairs features to names (for example, she can remember Mrs. Black by her black hair). This gives her a strategy to manage her discomfort and cope with the social interaction when she is encountering new relationships. At this point she is used to these things and just tells people she has trouble recalling faces, asking them to remind her where they have met before. That is an awakened brain.

Examples of the awe-inspiring power of neuroplasticity are obvious in children. As they grow in developing new skills, new connections are being made daily. When the first child in a family speaks or walks for the first time, it is a big deal and everyone hears about it. Seeing the brain grow before your very eyes is a magical experience. However, as the other children come along and new skills are popping up regularly for each of them, there is often little or no recognition. It becomes the normal course of events. Then we start to miss out on the magic happening every day.

Stories like Barbara's demonstrate just how much has changed in our understanding of brain function and its possibilities. The brain was once thought to be fairly static. We were told we were born with all the neurons we would ever have and that they were dying off as we aged. This is emphatically not true. Now we know that our thinking and awareness expands as we grow new neurons stimulated by chemistry produced by physical exercise. Thanks to neuroplasticity, our experiences and thoughts connect the dots to form new neural networks all the time.

Neuroplasticity Has an Upside and a Downside

Anything we keep doing over and over builds a stronger base in the brain and will more likely become an automatic response. This principle of automaticity works for us when it comes to repeatedly practicing skills in sports or playing an instrument. Or it can work against us when we repeatedly engage in behavior that quells anxiety but then has negative side effects in the long run. These are more often called addictions. These behaviors start out because your brain is reacting with anxiety to warn and protect you. When these emotions are so strong that you can no longer control your response, you are being hijacked by your nervous system. Spontaneous emotions are taking over without your having choice in the matter. The outcome is determined by whatever action you decide to take next. Addictions begin as a way of feeling better but can turn into a bigger problem than the one they solved. Lots of people with addictions don't realize they have a choice.

Thanks to recent research, all addictions are now being linked to the pleasure centers in the brain. When the social pressure gets to be too much and alcohol or drugs reduce the anxiety, making relationships or events more enjoyable, there is a neurobiological shift going on. The neurotransmitter dopamine is being released in the brain's pleasure center. A powerful surge of dopamine can come from many sources. Using nicotine, alcohol, drugs, food, sex, money, or any of the many sources of pleasure can all provide relief.

The problem surfaces when enjoying turns into craving. When social function cannot be enjoyed without the addiction of choice, the brain is out of balance and developing a dependency on the addiction. Because the pleasure center, where the uplifting dopamine is released, is located near regions for learning, memory, planning, and initiating and executing desires, many parts of the brain can readily be entrained to engage in addictive behavior, and then we become physically dependent.

The principles of neuroplasticity that enable our brains to adapt and engage new skills are now strengthening a habit that is no longer beneficial. Habits that most rapidly trigger the rush of pleasure from dopamine have proven to more likely become an addiction where cravings and dependency increase. The faster the delivery of pleasure, the more likely the brain will orient to that source of relief again. When we reach for relief from anxiety, we usually have no idea where that practice will lead or what we are training our brains to repeat in the future. When wanting becomes needing, you are in over your head and your body's anxiety is telling you to slow down. By allowing your nervous system to adjust slowly, there is an adaptation enabling the nervous system to grow new stable connections and expand its function. You want to know the outcome of your choices, thinking about the big picture, not just relief in the moment.

Neurochoice: Bringing About Brain Change through Choice

As a clinical neuropsychologist, I promote change in the brain by guiding normal people to expand the skills they need to fulfill their goals and by treating developmental disorders like dyslexia and acquired disorders like traumatic brain injury. When the neuropsychological testing reveals how a learning disorder has manifested in a person's cognitive style or how an injury to the brain has altered information processing, it is possible to design a treatment to strengthen those absent or lost abilities. The brain can heal, reorganize, and adapt to the demands presented. The restructuring of neural networks with new knowledge and experience happens all the time. Dyslexics learn to read, addicts get sober, cripples walk—all because they decided on the intention they would align with their passion and then, with guidance on what to do, put one foot in front of the other every day, just like Siddhartha.

At significant moments of change, I have had the image of my life as a tapestry, and the people, events, and experiences as threads woven in to influence and ultimately shape who I have become. A significant dimension of the tapestry is my genetics and the people, community, and thinking that surrounded me when I arrived as a child. This is the world I was given. Then there are my choices of friends, interests, training, attitudes, and standards to live by. Some combination of these makes up the person I have become. As I age and grow in insight, I have greater and greater influence over my thoughts, emotions, and behavior. I have more and more opportunity to decide what new threads I want woven into the tapestry of my life, which will shape how I experience the world and my life and what impact I will have because I have been here. The same applies to you. You can live your life seeking greater and greater awareness of the implications of your choices, and you can create the life you want. By growing in knowledge of your own brain, how it works, and the thoughts, emotions, beliefs, and meaning you can develop and utilize, you will awaken to your life.

There is not, as yet, consistent use of language to describe our inner world. I like to think that my mind or awareness or life force or spirit (choose a word you like) makes choices that manage my brain and nervous system. I am now able to fast as Siddhartha did, and my bodily desires do not run the show. I am now able to stop and think most of the time, instead of reacting. I can quiet my mind by using numerous methods to shut off the incessant chatter that would be there otherwise. Focusing on something soothing, like the soft sounds of music or a serene image, is like having a mantra without words to occupy my attention until those overly stimulated language neurons slow down and end the unwanted chatter of conversation. What I have learned in the convent and in neuropsychology is that changing my criterion for my behavior from reaction to chosen action is part of the awakening of the brain. The ability to recognize the outside reality and relate to it, but live from the inside vision guiding my actions, is the capacity of the awakened brain that I strive for daily. An awakened brain and an awakened life means living from the inside vision of life desired, regardless of the outside circumstances. When the inner reality is stronger and more real than the outer reality and you can act from your choice, you are entraining your brain and creating your life.

The concept of the awakened brain allows me to delve into my knowledge and observations of the human brain and the human potential for continuously reaching elevated states of consciousness. The term "awakened" usually refers to spiritually transcendent and peak experiences. *Awakened* is a word often used for mystics and the enlightened. Saints and sages have guided us into this realm for centuries. However, small steps and the daily realizations are going on all the time, expanding your awareness when you least realize. Since my discovery of neuropsychology, I have been weaving together insights gained through spiritual experiences and the brain function that processes that expansion of consciousness. In essence, the capacity for continued awakening is virtually limitless. The brain is constantly adapting and changing in its physical structure and chemical makeup in order to process the experience with which it is presented.

Past concepts of the brain described it as static at best and, at worst, dying off over the course of life. The newer research—and my clinical work with people interested in improving their brain function—shows us the opposite. My patients come to me for a variety of reasons. Some are making decisions that will alter their future, like investing in more education or choosing a new career path, and they want more information about themselves to ensure happiness and success. A neuropsychological evaluation will tell them which brain-processing skills they can count on for success and which ones might not help them reach their goal. From there they can decide to acquire new skills or consider different goals. These patients are not taking the trial-and-error approach because they don't want to have to deal with the "error." They are coming from a place in themselves of expecting to find the information they need for success. They are paving the road they anticipate traveling by learning about themselves and are building skills, before the fact, to ensure success in reaching their goal.

Some patients come to me because they have encountered obstacles along their chosen path and are seeking insight into their cognitive style and direction for building skills that will enable them to master the current challenge. This can be a child who is floundering in school or an adult who has not passed the licensing exam for their profession in medicine, law, or other fields. Many people who do well practicing their trade have trouble passing the written exam to get certified or licensed. Here, a life obstacle has drawn their attention to the need for growth, change, and expansion of their awareness of their brain and how they use it. Knowing how the brain works and what information is available about one's unique cognitive style, as well as the power to develop the brain's skills and abilities, has enabled many to make neuroplasticity work for them.

Finally, there have been those who have come for testing and treatment because they ran into an obstacle that has thrown them completely off their life's path. These are the people who have fallen down the stairs, ruptured a blood vessel, been injured in war or in a motor vehicle crash, collided with an object or person in a sports event, were stopped by loss of oxygen, or were slowed down by chemotherapy. There are numerous ways that an injury to the brain can result in a loss of function. Those with the drive, will, and purpose use the injury as an opportunity to not only recover function but to expand their meaning and purpose in life.

Bridget, an emergency room nurse who suffered a brain injury in a car crash, told me years after the accident that she would do it all over again because of all she had learned through her brain injury and all those she had helped as a result of her trauma. She is coming from a place within herself where she expects to be guided to a purposeful and fulfilling life, even after a brain injury. Martin, a triathlete who was hit by a car on his bike, told me that the brain injury was the best thing that ever happened to him. Before the injury, he reacted to events in his life. He is now awake to his choices and living a life he is creating.

As a first-generation neuropsychologist, there are many things I was originally taught that have turned out to be wrong. It has been these courageous and determined people who have taught me what is truly possible for the brain, and I suspect that journey will be never-ending as the human species continues to evolve. All these years in neuropsychology, I have consistently seen people in every walk of life, including some very prominent people, go through this "dark night" and come out with even greater light and joy.

Each of these people has learned to make a neurochoice, a word I use in an attempt to develop language for the expanding awareness that is coming forth about the power we have to influence the development of our brains. When you are aware of how a choice you make will impact your brain in the future, you are awake to influencing your own development. You really do have the ability to invent or reinvent yourself. You have choices about the thoughts you think, the emotions you feel, the words you speak, and the actions you take. Each of these dimensions of your experience influences the likelihood of your repeating your choice in the future. It's up to you, for you.

Since all we have is the present moment, we can talk about the brain from the perspective of each new aha moment that leads to an expansion of awareness. If we are mindful of our inner process, this is the moment of becoming awakened. However, when we observe ourselves from a longitudinal view, including ways we have grown in the past and expect to grow in the future, we must more accurately talk about the ever-awakening brain. This includes the expansion of our skills and our awareness. Each life experience contributes to our waking up to a broader perspective on what life is about. Depending on how we are focusing our awakened brain—on the neurochoices we are making—our skills can be broadening, deepening, and ever growing.

Developing a Buddha Brain

As a person who likes the comfort of well-established routines, I know it is important for me to continually ask myself if I am engaged in my life or if I'm going through the motions, seeking diversions and entertainment to tolerate what I am doing. Am I authentically engaging with the people in my life? Is there a purpose for what I do? Unfortunately, most of us focus on the doing and wonder why we are not happy when we succeed in achieving the goal. Happiness comes in the meaning we bring to what we are doing.

Years ago I came across a story of three stonecutters who spend the days of their lives cutting stones to build a cathedral.

Each was asked one question: "What are you doing?" The first responded, "I am cutting stones one foot by one foot by three-fourths of a foot. It is the only skill I have, so I will be here doing nothing but this for the rest of my life." The second stonecutter answered, "I am cutting stones one foot by one foot by three-fourths of a foot. This is how I earn a living to provide a warm home, food, and clothing for the wife I love and my beautiful children so that I can enjoy the love of my life and see my children grow healthy and happy." The third stonecutter answered, "I am cutting stones one foot by one foot by three-fourths of a foot. I have been blessed to be a part of the creation of this magnificent cathedral that is becoming a spiritual source of inspiration and will stand for hundreds of years, healing and inspiring those who come to search the depths of the soul."

After hearing this story, I had to stop and ask myself, "What am I doing?" No one can answer that but me. Am I going through the motions of life or doing what is expected by others? What is the meaning behind my action? Why do I do what I do? Are my inner peace, satisfaction, and well-being a part of the equation? What are the values, morals, and meanings that comprise the map I have constructed about how the world works and where I want to be within it? Is my life (and the networks in my brain that produce my perceptions and experience) being constructed by choice or by chance?

When the brain is entrained into an addiction, habit takes over and choice goes away. Without choice and the emotional, social, or spiritual reason for acting on the decision, meaning is not possible. Without meaning, life is devoid of the richness of the inner world that makes it worth living. With addictions, the habit consumes the consciousness, the bodily cravings dominate awareness, and life loses its richness.

However, when daily habits include activities that promote brain stability and growth, life gets to be very different. We now know that we are training our brains with everything we do. By having a balance during the day where stimulation and activity are stabilized by and interspersed with quiet and peace, the brain gets an opportunity to integrate and achieve a power of choice.

Certain practices like meditation are now being studied as neuroscience approaches questions about expanding consciousness. Meditation has been observed to be very powerful in strengthening the neural structures that control your focus. In fact, different forms of meditation strengthen different parts of your brain. Depending on whether the meditation practice is primarily language-based (such as mantras), sensory-based (such as walking meditations), or visual in nature (such as meditating on images), different parts of your brain are activated. And your brain needs balance. For example, if mind chatter is preventing you from focusing, meditating with a mantra might not be the best choice for you that day. Shifting out of language and into a sensory- or visual-based meditation would give the language neural structures a chance to stop rather than giving them more to compete with. The beauty of neurochoice is that now that you know this about your brain, you can choose your practice, rather than letting your brain take you somewhere you don't want to go. (See the Awakening Applications for more meditation suggestions.)

This is the upside of neuroplasticity. The nuns and monks who meditate every day exercise their brains to establish the control of focused attention, which produces the insight, wisdom, and compassion we seek in them. Through their spiritual practices, they are developing and strengthening their focus, which leads them to be happier, more fulfilled people. They make sure to ground themselves daily in practices and activities that stabilize their emotions and connect them with inspiration—hallmarks of a Buddha Brain.[3]

But a monastery or convent is not the only answer to the quest for peace, wholeness, and fulfillment. Mindfulness meditation, focusing on the present moment, yoga, and other practices also cultivate a physiology that promotes inner peace. These activities entrain the brain as well, giving us access to the upside of neuroplasticity. The expanding capacity to reflect on events and what they mean in your life allows you to develop insight into the richness of the experience and the implications for who you want to be.

We now know how to do it, but are we making those choices or are we living by default? Mostly, what I have observed is that people do not understand that they are entraining their brain with the activities they are experiencing—and then they wonder why they are struggling with unwanted emotions, thoughts, and habits. That is why I am writing this book. All of us want to feel better and are interested in how to get there. The revelations coming from neuropsychology and neuroscience are showing us new ways to take charge of our own experience.

The Brain Repeats What It Knows

There are many extreme environments on our planet that have created unique conditions, shaping the brains of the young from birth. Some of them have been pretty unwanted and traumatic. Whole generations have been born and raised in Northern Ireland knowing nothing but violence. Children in Africa are now raised only by grandparents or orphaned because of AIDS. The drug war in Mexico is creating another generation that has come into this world surrounded by violence and orphaned as well. When I consider the huge challenges faced by these children, as well as those who have suffered in Afghanistan or on Native American reservations or those whose families survived the holocausts in Germany, Cambodia, and Rwanda, my heart goes out to them. The Buddhist prayer "May all beings know loving-kindness" comes to mind. Their brains are being trained from birth in a way very different from those who live in stable environments. How will they see our world? Will they have a passion for peace, creating a world they long for? Or will they repeat the violence they were born into?

When we look back in history, it is often out of such tragedy that great innovation arises. The enormous suffering observed by Siddhartha called him from the comforts of his magnificent home, where every desire was satisfied, and guided him to the inner world of his own experience. He left his father's palace to free himself of all possessions and comforts and explore his own experience. He came from a place within himself where the impossible was possible, and he persisted until he succeeded in becoming the Buddha we know. Many noted figures in history have done this—great saints, healers, and teachers. In the Christian tradition, this is the same story as St. Francis of Assisi, who was born to a privileged environment and gave it all up for a rich spiritual inner world and the opportunity to serve others.

Siddhartha and Francis intuitively comprehended the power of neuroplasticity even then. Siddhartha declared that he would achieve the capacity to fast and no longer be driven by the cravings of his body. This freed him and awakened his brain to an awareness of the inner peace that was possible if he let go of craving and desires. Siddhartha's determination to find freedom from suffering led him to meditate and release all focus on his cravings until they left him in peace, no longer active and causing him suffering. We now think of this as dismantling a neural network. Siddhartha created the first Buddha Brain, aware of the ability to be free of physical dependency. The word Buddha literally means "awakened one." Reacting to the suffering he observed in the world, Siddhartha persisted in awakening his own brain, freeing himself from the suffering he felt, and has conveyed that awareness to millions who have also sought their own Buddha Brain.

As I consider Siddhartha's accomplishment, my thoughts wander to an awareness that the brain is simply an organ that repeats what it knows. If drugs or alcohol provide relief from suffering, the brain searches for more of this relief. If fighting sustains survival, the adrenaline automatically surges forth. We are creatures of habit because that is the nature of the mechanisms in the brain and body. Our repeated behavior shapes our experience of the world and triggers neural mechanisms for our reactions. We don't always know when we are engaging the upside of neural plasticity or the downside. Sometimes a painkiller prescribed by the doctor is a great blessing. Sometimes people look back at that moment and see the beginning of a nightmare of addiction. We may start out with good intentions and later find ourselves where we least expected to be.

One of the questions frequently considered in my office has to do with who is particularly vulnerable to the new addiction we see developing with technology. When does technology switch from being an asset to a liability? Unfortunately, the answers to questions like this are generally answered in retrospect, when we more clearly see just what has happened. When young people come in for an evaluation because college did not work out or grades are not what they were, stories unfold of emotional and sexual needs being satisfied on the internet at the price of educational achievement and social development.

Particularly vulnerable are the very sensitive or socially awkward. Some may have cognitive deficits in social and emotional information processing. Some have prosopagnosia, or the inability to recognize and remember faces, like Barbara. Their enormous sensitivity makes it hard to roll with life's emotional ups and downs. The lack of awareness of social cues, conversational innuendo, or body language is based in how their brains process information. We know all addictions are habits our brain and body believe will make us feel better. Vulnerable people escape into habits that provide relief, not realizing what else comes with the package. Some people have created the automatic neural network that focuses on feeling better in the short term but have ignored the consequences of their behavior. However, they have options. You can dismantle the neural networks, delivering unwanted behavior, and build new, more functional automatic habits, just like Siddhartha did. Going from an addict brain to a Buddha Brain is a journey available to everyone.

Kids who are highly emotional, sensitive, or reactive or those with Asperger's Disorder or a general social ineptness can be taught how to navigate the world slowly, one encounter at a time. Sometimes, social skills are explained in the social interactions found in stories and videos, which is actually where we learn a lot. Without being guided by parents or therapists or observing scenarios seen in the movies where the ending reveals "how it all turned out," many kids are at a loss when entering the social scene. A few spontaneous social "mistakes," resulting in embarrassment, put a damper on those efforts. However, escaping into the emotional stability and safety of "iToys" often creates a new problem on top of the original one.

As a young man, Siddhartha had all of life's comforts and was protected from the strife of the masses. He was privileged and gifted, but his heart went out to those he saw suffering. The passion to find an answer and lead the way for freedom from suffering moved him to explore inner realms of human existence. He sought meaning in his life and had the ability and passion to sustain his efforts. The things we care about, which activate the pleasure centers of the brain to make life worth living, can come from the heart and the brain together. By finding a purpose that contributes to both ourselves and others, we can create a life where the efforts that go out from us return to us.

Keeping a Buddha Brain in the Modern Day

Each new generation and new age must address the negative consequences that creep up on them when they live life by reacting instead of acting. The technology generation is beginning to demonstrate some of their challenges with addictive behavior, as we have seen throughout history when there is an availability of new sources of pleasure. In the past thirty to forty years, our world has steadily speeded up. Radios, telephones, and television were conveniences and entertainment, enhancing our awareness and quality of life. Now it seems that technology has been woven into the core fabric of our lives. "How did we live without cell phones?" is a common comment as instantaneous communication moves our world forward faster and faster. But what is this change in our environment doing to our brains? Our senses are bombarded with information, and we must decide if we will automatically follow the stream of associations or decide which of it contributes to our well-being. When the amount of stimulation to the brain exceeds its comfort level, anxiety increases to warn us of imbalance.

As wonderful as it is to have information at our fingertips, it is shaping us in ways we are only just glimpsing and creating new addictions never seen before. When I was trained and licensed as a psychologist, there was no such thing in our general population as a checking disorder, which is characterized by the need to constantly check messages. There were people with Obsessive Compulsive Disorder (OCD) who experienced so much anxiety from their thoughts that they had to go back to see if the stove was turned off or the door locked to achieve some inner peace. But now we have a brand-new mainstream version of OCD blossoming in our younger generation and moving deeper and deeper into our wider society. Now we feel the need to check our messages all day from many forms of technology. The rush of pleasure when the desired message finally arrives has grabbed the memory and pleasure centers of many brains, producing the "need" to check for messages. Technology has made lots of life much simpler and more easily managed. But how do we know when technology is enhancing life or taking over?

Our children and young adults, who have known no other world than the current environment of immediate gratification of tech tools, are being shaped by them. Pediatricians are concerned about the effect that the immediate gratification of technology has on the forming brains of young children. They recommend that parents refrain from giving their kids iToys until they are at least two years old. We do not know how those little brains are being trained by the stimulation of the dopamine rush that results from such an immediate response, but most who discuss this agree that it should be a first priority to connect kids to parents and family, showing them how to value and understand people, relationships, and emotions over withdrawal into the tech world.

Like all innovation, lots of good has come from technology. Kids who have moved away are still in touch with old friends. Homework information is at their fingertips. Loneliness is abated by the instantaneous ability to "reach out" (even if you are not actually touching anyone). But recent research suggests the problems of addiction are surfacing. Researchers are now talking about the effects of technology on the iBrain, which is showing some unique vulnerabilities when bombarded with that dopamine rush of immediate gratification. When technology takes hold, a digital social addiction can result. What started out as a convenience, with email replacing snail mail, has become habit with IM-ing, texting, tweeting, pinging, and poking. Research suggests that all these practices set off the gratifying release of dopamine in the reward centers of the iBrain. Whether they become a digital social addiction or not is the question. Are people checking to achieve a purpose, or must they do so to avoid the anxiety that is being triggered by these trained instinctive habits? How is technology enhancing the quality of our lives and how is it detracting from it? How do you know when enjoyment is turning into craving? And what do you do about it?

So far we see signs of trouble developing in those who lose sleep over keeping up with emails and social network sites. Some people are in the habit of checking email and social network sites in the morning before getting dressed or in the middle of the night. This puts the iHabit before sleep and health, which is not sustainable. Kids are sleeping with their cell phones, BlackBerrys, and laptops to "stay connected." Procrastination with work, school, and home activities are a warning sign that iTools are taking over.

Having a number of friends who are real, physically in front of you, available to be seen with your eyes, heard with your ears, and even hugged with your arms—versus a list of names on Facebook—is a better measure of the individual's current atmosphere. Certainly, the number of hours a day spent on technology, surfing, trolling, and obsessing over your current status suggests the strength of the iNeural network that has developed in your brain. The "need to know" your number of hits, results, or friends as a measure of your worth and the anxiety this causes, especially if the call is dropped, internet is down, or the computer crashes, all tell us who remains in charge and who is being run by the iTools.

Is this the tip of the iceberg? Technology is unquestionably addictive. It responds to your command, gives you what you want immediately and without an argument, goes at your pace, and gives you those delicious rushes of pleasure. iTools easily entrain your brain to expect to have your curiosity satisfied. But is the tool created to serve our needs and interests becoming the master?

For those who are hooked, it has now become more like the challenge we face with addictions to food. You can't just stop cold turkey. Food is necessary for life, and technology is quickly becoming woven into the very fabric of our world in education, the workplace, and the home. What is one to do once hooked on daily hours of Facebook or a passion for online games and comics? Is what was once an advantage and convenience now becoming a shackle?

For the past forty years, the world has been developing a technology that has become the single most powerful tool the planet has ever seen. We now transcend time and space communicating around the globe. The influence of technology also contains the single most addictive characteristics for the human brain, providing that lightning-speed rush of dopamine. As the world changes with more and more new stimulation coming at us daily, our brains continue to respond and evolve. The change is inevitable. The only question is which way it will go. Are you reacting or choosing an action? Will your change be by choice or by chance?

As I reflect on the enormous change that has happened in the world during my lifetime, it makes me wonder whether I can even understand what people growing up in the age of technology are experiencing. I tend to doubt I can. With that thought, I also feel very blessed to have had the simpler life, with a parochial education and three years of silence as a young adult in the convent, to ground me in an inner world from which I can observe and engage in my experience. Because of that, I have been aware that with each major loss of the "givens" in my life, I have had to choose the life I want and consider where that choice will take me. Leaving home for the convent, leaving the convent to create my own life, choosing an education and a career—the list goes on and on. If we take the opportunity between career choices and relationships, or after our parents are gone, to observe who we are now, we knit together the tapestry of our lives, bringing the meaning and purpose we desire to our choices. From there, we view our accomplishments and consider which next step would be most fulfilling.

Does the speed of our technological world distract us from neurochoice, the most important power we have for influencing our own quality of life? Are we really making a choice as we react to all the daily stimulation? Do we have awareness of where these reactions are taking us? Do we even know what our choices are?

Like any innovation, the long-term pattern of the influences surfaces slowly over time. Neurochoice, the awareness of the impact of our life choices on our neuropsychological development, is at the heart of our challenge in the technological age.

The Brain's Garden:
A Way to Cultivate Healthy Behaviors

The ever-changing nature of the brain easily lends itself to a garden theme. As you take the concepts of this chapter and apply them to your own life, think of the sprouting, fertilizing, and pruning going on within your neural network. These concepts show us not only the inside picture of how healthy brains change but also how the brain physically heals and adapts after an injury to restore lost cognitive, behavioral, and social functioning. This is also true of developing brains. Barbara's story showed that a child's brain can be engaged in precise tasks that entrain neuronal structures and produce stronger ability.

The same is true for adults seeking new skills. At age sixty-five, I had to learn to connect my thoughts to my fingers and then master word processing in order to write this book. It took repeated effort over time, but now I am not limited to paper and pen, and my fingers know their way around the keyboard as thoughts come in their direction. Essentially, I am observing that the notion of what aging looked like when I was growing up has vastly changed for the better. The brain is "use it or lose it," and now we know the mechanisms that keep the system humming over time.

These activities spark the growth of new neurons, a process known as sprouting. In graduate school I was taught that the brain cannot grow new cells. Not true! The process called neurogenesis enables the brain to keep changing throughout life by producing new cells, or individual neurons. As new neurons grow, they engage with the existing neural organization of the brain, further expanding the present neural networks. We now know there are specific triggers that turn on the brain's capacity for growth and development. Sprouting is triggered by the fertilizer of brain-derived neurotrophic factor (BDNF), which is a kind of chemistry activated by physical exercise. When you are feeling those little aches and pains after exercising, it means that you have actually activated an inflammatory process that activates the chemical for new cell growth. The expansion of interest in exercise, such as working with a trainer or participating in community athletic events like walks or runs or swims, contributes to the growth of new neurons in your brain.

Some of the other triggers that activate healthy brain function include regular intellectual stimulation that provides a workout for strengthening cognitive skills. The more you use the neural networks of your skills, the stronger they get. Then, taking those cognitive skills into a social setting connects them to emotional and social awareness. Frequent social engagement offers many opportunities for activating the complex brain functions of recognizing emotional experience, using social skills, and engaging in language use.

Pruning is also a neurological term referring to the decrease in neuron density due to lack of stimulation. Loss of a function can occur when we no longer use skills once developed. This is seen when we no longer play a favorite sport for many years or when we no longer speak a second language learned in childhood. Hence, sometimes pruning occurs and represents an undesirable loss. However, sometimes pruning can be an advantage when it enables us to overcome patterns of behavior that are dysfunctional and break bad habits that have limited our lives, like addictions. In either case, neuroplasticity represents these adaptations of the brain.

I recently had the delightful experience of seeing a woman who had come to me for treatment of a brain injury ten years prior. The injury had been the result of a freak accident in which she'd experienced a blow to the back of her head by a falling object. She was significantly cognitively impaired but had overcome many huge obstacles in her life prior to the injury and was open to the possibility that she could overcome the limits of the brain injury too. Her treatment was slow but produced consistent progress, and she eventually moved on to a new lifestyle she enjoyed. On this occasion of her return to see me, she was exploring a particular challenge and sought the benefit of all the knowledge of her brain she had grown to trust.

As we concluded the session, having sorted out an option she felt comfortable with, she spontaneously asked for a piece of paper to make some notes summarizing our conversation, as her memory capacity fluctuates with her fatigue. What was surprising to me was not that she had returned to utilize my services nor that she had requested a piece of paper. What was surprising to me was that she sat writing notes while simultaneously listening to my words and commenting about her decisions. Although she had made great progress in treatment, I had never seen her be able to multitask by writing, listening, and talking all at the same time in the ten years I had known her. When I pointed this out to her, she had been totally unaware of it, and we both laughed, marveling at this continual expansion of the brain's skills when we keep using them.

Now, this might sound like a small accomplishment, but trust me, it is not small. The ability to do more than one thing at a time puts us in a completely different league of functioning, with exponentially greater opportunities available. This woman's garden was certainly blossoming. Despite how marvelous and satisfying it is for me to journey with someone along that path of expansion toward the fullness of life it offers, the really compelling issue for me has to do with the spirit, drive, desire, expectations, and developing consciousness of the people who overcome enormous odds, in contrast to the people who do not achieve recovery or mastery of skills that appear to be easily within their grasp.

When it comes to recovering from brain injury or addictions, overcoming a learning disability, or developing a key skill, there is much more than the engagement of the functions of the neurological structures of the brain. I'm most intrigued by the awakening part of the journey, observing the expansion of consciousness that enables choice and change. When we can envision a possibility that does not yet exist and have the belief to embrace that possibility and expect to see it manifest in our lives, we are living in a truly flourishing garden.

In my career, I have observed the incredible power of the human spirit and consciousness over the physical mechanisms of the body and brain. I have been honored to participate in that sacred, transformative journey with hundreds of people over the course of my life and have great appreciation for all they have taught me. The facts and theory I have learned are the basis for my professional services. The KNOWING about what is possible is a result of my observing courageous, committed people who would not be stopped by the physical limitations or the prevailing consciousness. Their stories about the brain and belief can be an inspiration as you, too, direct the sprouting and pruning within.

The brain is truly like a garden. The flowers that will blossom are the ones you tend to and cultivate. In this way, you will direct the changes within your own brain, rather than leaving it to chance.

Awakening Applications

• Because of neuroplasticity—the brain's ability to form new neural connections—change within the brain is inevitable. You can leave that change to chance or influence it through the use of neurochoice.

• Repetition increases the likelihood that thoughts, behaviors, and emotions will become automatic. Healthy habits and addictions are both formed this way. What thoughts, actions, or emotions do you repeat day in and day out? Are you consciously choosing them so that they serve you? Or has choice gone away to the point that they have become addictions? Observe your habits over the course of a week and evaluate whether they are serving you and creating meaning in your life. If not, start using conscious choice to form the healthy habits you want.

• One way to make neuroplasticity work for you is through meditation. A meditation practice entrains the brain to give you greater control over your choice of thoughts and releases the nervous system from your normal state to create greater harmony. Choose your practice to create the balance you need.

- For a sensory form of meditation, try walking in a quiet, peaceful setting. Notice the sensations that greet you, from the feel of the breeze to the scents, sounds, and sights. Observe them without judgment and then let go of thoughts that come to you.

- For a language-based meditation, choose a mantra. Mantras can be a word that represents what you want more of (for example, "calm" or "peace") or a longer phrase. Think or speak the words in time with your breath.

- For a visual-based meditation, find an image or piece of artwork that makes you feel good and has special meaning to you. Gaze at it while breathing slowly. If thoughts pop up, let them come and go, observing them without judgment.

♦ To keep a Buddha Brain in a world dominated by technology, remember your power of choice. Are you mindlessly reacting to the tech noise in front of you, or are you choosing to interact with it, with awareness of how your choices affect your life? Awareness makes all the difference.

♦ It is important to tend to your brain's garden to cultivate healthy behaviors. In addition to exercise, there are other ways to add fertilizer to sprouting neurons. First, a healthy diet provides the brain with adequate nutrition for thriving and accessing potential. Protein, omega-3s, herbs, and natural sugars all promote mental clarity. Sleep is a restorative time for the brain, and achieving the rejuvenating balance of activity and rest on a regular basis enhances the brain's capacity to function under all conditions. Finally, because medical conditions such as diabetes, obesity, and depression create an unhealthy climate for the brain, managing your physical health is essential for brain health. See the Resources section on my website, awakeningthebrain.com, for further reading on these topics.

Notes

1. Katherine Harmon, "New MRI Maps Assess Connectivity to Establish 'Brain Age' Curve for Children and Adults," *Scientific American*, http://blogs.scientificamerican.com/observations/2010/09/09/new-mri-maps-assess-connectivity-to-establish-brain-age-curve-for-children-and-adults/(accessed 10/24/11).

2. Donald Hebb, *The Organization of Behavior* (New York: John Wiley & Sons, 1949).

3. Rick Hanson and Richard Mendius, *Buddha's Brain* (Oakland, CA: New Harbinger Publications, 2009).

3

How Knowledge from Neuropsychology Informs Belief

Belief is a powerful force for bringing about the outcomes you desire. But sometimes, by itself, belief won't get you all the way there. I think of neuropsychology as a key that unlocks the promise held in a belief. That is because neuropsychology gives you knowledge about the mechanisms within your brain, the options available to you, and the choices you can make that will manifest your belief. Once you know how attention is controlled, how your brain regulates emotions, and what you can do to influence these processes, you have the knowledge that gives belief its power. With informed belief, you can go further than you'd ever thought possible. Knowledge is what makes the dream become reality.

Neuropsychology is a relatively new field that started in the '70s. I was blessed to enter it at the beginning. This gift is, of course, a double-edged sword, since the excitement of new beginnings is often countered by the frustration of not having the answers you need for the people you serve. Nonetheless, being involved in a developing field requires all the same skills of belief, vision, and persistence that this book is about, and my career is one of the ways I expanded my understanding of belief.

Neuropsychology is a field of knowledge about how the brain affects human function and how you can increase your brain's effectiveness. In other words, neuropsychologists can measure cognitive, emotional, social, and personality characteristics and see how they interact to make up the person that is you. Then, if the insight derived inspires you to action, there are a multitude of steps that can be taken to adapt or change any of these characteristics. It's all up to you. The brain is the mechanism that executes your choices, and it is a very adaptable organ. Neuropsychology is the professional discipline focused on describing the brain functions we have and offering methods for developing or eliminating them as you choose. In the years I have been engaged in this discipline, I have been in awe of the amazing potential I have witnessed in ordinary people who decided to change their circumstances and have succeeded beyond our wildest imagining.

NEUROPSYCHOLOGICAL ASSESSMENT MEASURES THE FOLLOWING:

Intelligence	Executive functions
Language (expressive, receptive)	Memory
Visuo-spatial skills	Sensory and motor skills
Constructional skills	Academic achievement
Attentional control	Psychological development

Options Revealed through Neuroscientific Discoveries

Neuroscience studies specific brain structures and interprets their function and interaction with our other parts. Many other professional disciplines contribute to the discoveries in this field of study, which contains a broad spectrum of scientists from disciplines including neurology, radiology, biology, and psychiatry. From my perspective, they are all writing about neuropsychology, the interface between physical, neurological structures, and the psyche. As we discover the characteristics of the brain and the mechanisms for its expansion, our consciousness about the outcomes of our actions expands. Our options are revealed. Neurochoice, a choice based on the intention to expand neuropsychological ability, is now possible. Many neuroscientists actually call themselves neuropsychologists and write papers on neuropsychology because this is an interface for integration.

Why would I bother to make this point? Because the definition of the word *neuropsychology* combines our essential dimensions. *Neuro* obviously refers to the nervous system, including the brain and all the nerves that run through the body, regulating organs and functions. The actual definition of *psyche* is soul. From that definition, I think of the unique spirit or essence that gives life to each of us, embodying the brain and body we have to work with. *Ology* at the end of the word simply means "the study of." So, for me, neuropsychology is the study of the Life Force that is you, manifesting through your brain and body, influencing your development within the context of the family, community, and circumstances you are experiencing. The brain is shaped and reshaped moment by moment by all those experiences, which is why no two brains are the same.

Many innovative approaches are emerging to explore the fascinating questions about just how the brain processes and regulates our experience. Whole new divisions of neuroscience have recently been appearing in the neuroscience literature. One is called interpersonal neurobiology. Here the focus is on interpreting neuroscience to understand social and interpersonal interaction. This has offered groundbreaking concepts for understanding what the neuroscientific findings are telling us about ourselves. Another is called contemplative neuroscience, which involves studying the power of meditation on brain function. These neuroscientists often study the brains of nuns, monks, and anyone following a consistent spiritual practice to better understand the brain's mechanisms during meditation and prayer.

Every new landscape of discovery requires new terminology to describe the insights and concepts reflecting the outcomes. This is often helpful to prevent the brain from bringing along old meanings to color new concepts. The word *ipseity* has recently been used in discussing such studies in order to differentiate between our many dimensions that neuroscience is trying to understand. Ipseity refers to the essential nature of our existence, the bare awareness of the life force before the development of concepts, when there is an absence of a constructed self. It refers to the core self, the essence of being, before the constructs of the mind, brain, and personality are included. This might sound too abstract, but take a moment to consider this question: Which of your dimensions can observe your mind chattering away, your brain when it shuts down in a fog, or your personality when it rises to the occasion? Although we are in the beginning stages of exploring who we are in these many dimensions, the beginning is always establishing a language we can use to make observations and share experiences. Many new perspectives on the neuro-science findings are coming forth to offer interpretations of what it all means. I, too, am taking a stab at sharing what I have observed in the laboratory of my clinical office all these years. Over time you will discover the interpretations that work for you if you observe your own experiences and develop a vocabulary to discuss them.

Understanding how the brain works and how to work it in the innumerable different ways we observe is useful and life-enhancing information and the focus for everyone pursuing this knowledge. As a clinical neuropsychologist, I am skilled in methods of measuring human function and facilitating the process of change, adaptation, and growth on the path of our life journey. Many of the people who have come to my office with severe neurological limitations exhibited a relentless belief in their potential but lacked information on how they could do something to achieve the functionality they desired. Without knowledge of the neuro-psyche mechanisms and the options available to them for growth, healing, and specific skill development, they are groping in the dark, not knowing which direction to choose. They just don't know what their neurochoices are.

From a practical standpoint, what does that mean? The easiest example comes from applying the knowledge of neuropsychology to expanding children's learning capacity. My original interest after graduate school was in working with learning disabilities. Relentless mothers and teachers, who have children studying material and repetitively practicing skills, have shown for eons that persistence pays off. Some children master a skill the first time around, while others need consistent repetition before inde-pendent mastery kicks in.

As long as children have the innate potential, a reasonably accurate method, and a stable belief that they will achieve mastery of the skill, which enables them to persist, the desired outcome will manifest. Dyslexic children whose fathers have told them that Dad overcame a challenge with reading and that they can benefit from training are saved a lot of worry and wondering because they believe that reading is possible. This is how knowledge informs belief. We do it all the time. Science informs and shapes our beliefs and expectations. If we listen to the knowledge and act on a belief, life is enhanced.

A simple example from my own experience came when I first discovered the chemical basis for how exercise improves sleep and mood. This benefit was something I had experienced and known intuitively, but it became far more real, important, and prominent in my own choices for activities promoting well-being in my body when I grasped it conceptually. Now my career in neuropsychology is based on brain knowledge that informs my belief as I offer guidance to others who believe they can expand their skills. My challenge has been to figure out how to get these concepts across to others in a meaningful way so that they can benefit from the discoveries. As you begin to grasp the power you have to adapt your own brain and expand your skills, you will have neurochoices to select from and the ability to strengthen the skills you want.

Moving from Powerlessness to Comprehending a Believable Path

The best approach I have found for sharing all this knowledge is looking for the "teachable moment" when people are in touch with a challenge. When patients come to my practice for testing and treatment, I tell them that they will get their crash course in neuropsychology along the way. That information contains the perspective or consciousness needed to move from powerlessness and reactivity in relation to brain function, to comprehending a believable path for creating what they want. It is my hope that reading this book will engage you in thinking about your brain while you receive this mini crash course in neuropsychology.

As the field of neuropsychology expands, integrating the constantly expanding neuroscientific discoveries with psychological principles of human functioning, we can see more and more specifically how to nurture the potential within the brain. As the mechanisms of function are discovered and the principles that actualize potential are applied, our expanded potential is revealed. Discovery about ourselves is an exciting frontier. If you decide to explore your own cognitive style with the help of a neuropsychologist, you will find lots of neurochoices awaiting you in endless insights, tricks, and skills to expand your understanding and abilities.

As stated earlier, the perspective that I am developing here is an integration of brain and belief. From that perspective, I view science as a form of revelation. My definition of revelation has to do with inspired awareness that makes obvious knowledge based in belief. Science is, of course, the study of physical matter, and in the case of neuroscience, that study is focused on observing and describing the structures and functions of the brain and nervous system. Here the word *revelation* is used from a metaphysical, spiritual, and consciousness perspective. When the information from neuroscience enables our consciousness to grasp the complex functions of the brain, it is possible to make conscious neurochoices for how to apply, strengthen, or diminish those functions to serve the purpose of an intention. For example, when you learn about the ability to expand your vocabulary or extend your ability to focus and you see someone actually do it, a possibility is revealed that you can believe in with certainty. This is what I refer to as a revelation.

So what has been offered to people who have come and gone in my office over the years? Patients are given a crash course in neuropsychology so that they can know how to work with their own unique cognitive style and understand several specific structures in the brain and how they function to manifest their experience and behavior. Just consider that your brain is made up of 100 billion neurons, and those neurons all talk to each other through connections that we call neural networks. Each neuron has multiple branches, called dendrites, that extend from it so that it can communicate in many different directions. Scientists tell us that there are 100 trillion points of connection among neurons and dendrites in the human brain. It is hard to comprehend that all that is going on inside of me as I type these words.

Think about all this going on in your brain as you read these words while these 100 trillion connections, firing to direct your eyes along the page, process the visual information, convert it to meaning, and store it to memory. Step back and try to comprehend this amazing event happening in your head right now. My present consciousness accepts the truth of this information but cannot step back far enough to see it happening. We also know that each of those neurons is talking to the others by responding to an electrical impulse that activates chemicals that move from one neuron to another, carrying the messages I am sending with my thoughts and experiences.

As people coming for a neuropsychological evaluation take the tests, observe themselves doing the tasks, and gain insight into the style of their own brain with the help of a clinical interpretation of the findings, their crash course is establishing a new set of concepts about themselves. One of the functions of the frontal lobes is to establish and hold on to a set. This might be a sequence of steps required to perform a task like running the copy machine, or it might be a pattern of behavior developed for a specific social outcome. Learning about new ways of doing things and deciding to adapt your behavior because the outcome offers the improvements you desire is literally holding a new set in your brain and executing it in your life. When you make such an intention, establish the set, and make a choice to apply the knowledge, you are making a neurochoice and determining where within yourself you are coming from.

How Attention Is Controlled

A good starting point for grasping how all those neurons are organized into specific functions is in the frontal lobe, where a cluster of neurons called the cingulate resides (see Figure 3.1). The reason for choosing this as a starting point is because the cingulate controls the brain's ability to focus attention on your interest and sustain it there long enough to accomplish your intention. Being able to show up and stay with the task is the most essential skill—the first step. The cingulate is located in the center of the frontal lobes and receives input from many parts of the brain and the body.

Along with the ability to focus attention, the cingulate regulates the emotions we are aware of and want to monitor and manages our thoughts that are held in mind. The cingulate has been called the emotional regulator, the cortical regulator, and the executive operating officer. This is where you decide what you want to focus on or leave behind. The stronger your cingulate, the more control you have over your experience. When a person has a brain injury, the ability to control or sustain focus is typically weakened. Neuropsychological treatment, using cognitive rehabilitation, enables the person to engage in tasks that will strengthen the muscle of the cingulate to have greater accuracy (focused attention) and flexibility (alternating or divided attention) and to sustain effort of focus longer (sustained or silent attention).

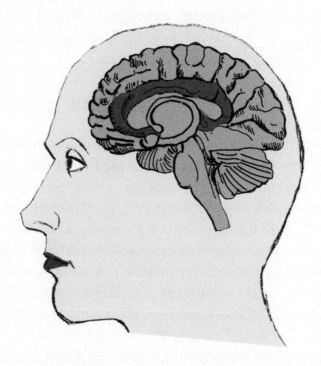

Figure 3.1 The cingulate: regulating focused attention

Neuroscience has demonstrated in recent years that there are a variety of practices that strengthen the cingulate and expand its functions for normal development. As psychology has shifted to explore human potential rather than pathology, studies of nuns and monks who have been meditating and exercising their cingulate for many years have taught us about these functions and the potential for expanding the functioning of any brain that so chooses. The more often you pause to observe your thoughts and emotions, rather than react and be your thoughts and emotions, the more you strengthen the cingulate and your ability to monitor and choose your actions. (See the Awakening Applications at the end of the chapter for more ways to strengthen your cingulate.)

ATTENTION TYPES

Focused and vigilant	Divided attention
Selective attending	Silent concentration
Alternating attention	

This control over your focus likewise enables you to decide how you want to relate to time. Do you want to live in the past with your memories? Do you want to focus on the present moment where you are now? Do you want to consider and imagine your future in an effort to create the life you want? Without choosing your focus of time, you are often at the mercy of the associations, sensations, and emotions that pop into your head and drag you off by default into a stream of thoughts and feelings that influence the present experience.

Now, there is nothing wrong with orienting to any one of these points in time if that is what you choose to do. The greater effectiveness, however, is in consciously choosing to go there rather than finding yourself there by default when the experience does not serve your purpose. If you focus on a vision for the future and take the time to sense the emotions that arise when you imagine the outcome, you may have a revelation as to whether that possibility is a good match for you. When you imagine a possibility, feelings of curiosity, interest, meaning, purpose, enthusiasm, excitement, hope, and desire are all indicators of future satisfaction. Similarly, focusing on an issue in the present helps to get to the heart of the matter, rather than continually responding impulsively or habitually and repeating old behaviors from the past that are not effective. We want to learn from and call on the beneficial knowledge acquired in the past but not live there by default because we are not aware that we have the option to move on. It's the difference between being controlled by unconscious habits and creating your life through the intention of your conscious belief.

Where Are Your Thoughts?

Now, let's consider the platform of thought that neuropsychology calls working memory. Working memory is a function of our frontal lobes, housed in two distinct locations (see Figures 3.2 and 3.3). Neuroscience has demonstrated a location in the left frontal lobe for holding and considering words. You are using it right now as you read this material and think about what it means to you. On the opposite side of your head, the right frontal lobe holds images you are thinking about. Here you may already be

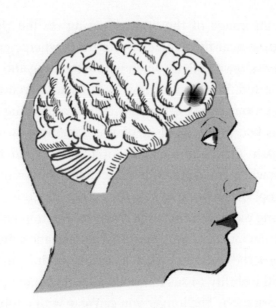

Figure 3.2 Working memory: right hemisphere for visuals

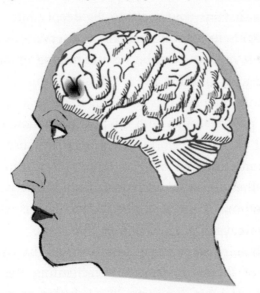

Figure 3.3 Working memory: left hemisphere for language

picturing an image of the brain focusing on the right, frontal, outer location near the temple of your head, where neuroscientific studies have shown activity when we are building and using visual images in mind. Working memory is the neuropsychological term used to describe activity in these locations for holding information in mind as you think about it. Working memory is where we do mental math, plan our schedule for the day, hold the map for directions when traveling, and refer to the shopping list. This is the "desktop" of the brain, where the action happens.

Working memory is also the space in which to collect data on a topic, review its meaning, consider its relevance, and decide on how to proceed. Awareness of a variety of information enters here, and the ability to sustain one's focus expands the space you have to work with. The longer you can stay with a topic, the more deeply and broadly you can explore its value and apply its implications. This sustains your focus to dig deeper into the meaning of your thoughts in working memory. Observations from events in the present moment can be held here long enough to glean their meaning. A common use for these neurons is the recall of memories from the past; this allows us to compare previous outcomes from past decisions with the possible outcomes of current decisions. It is called working memory because this is the platform upon which we hold multiple bits of information and think about them from an analytical, synthesizing perspective or from an emotional or spiritual perspective. This is where we take the data and weave it into a meaningful outcome.

Although spiritual practice is not usually discussed from the perspective of the brain functions facilitating the experience, there are lots of brain functions like working memory that are operative in spiritual experience and will be discussed in greater detail in later chapters. Working memory is essential for all our intentional experience. When we decide on a spiritual focus for our attention, working memory is the brain structure that holds in mind the words of the prayer or the sacred image or plays the inspiring tune in your head. You get to choose what goes on in there that you will pay attention to and create the experience you are having.

The depth and breadth of our capacity to reflect and mentally explore is largely influenced by the relationship between the cingulate, which sustains the focus, and working memory centers, which hold the volume of information to be considered. The longer the cingulate enables us to reflect, the deeper we can go on a topic. Similarly, working memory has two characteristics. One is volume, or how many bits of information can be held there, and the second is agility, or how accurately we can manipulate or juggle the proverbial balls filling the air. This is where mental math is calculated for making correct change, if the numbers don't get away from you in the process. How far we get and how well we will do with manipulating and integrating information is largely affected by the strength of the relationship between the cingulate and working memory centers in the frontal lobe.

Adding Emotional Information

Working memory is also where we consider the bigger questions of our lives when emotion is an important part of the decision-making formula. With some decisions, we use our imagination to try on possible actions and outcomes to see how they feel. Here, your reasoning ability in your frontal lobes is calling on the information of emotion to see, through imagination, what discerning contribution comes from the knowledge expressed by your limbic system (see Figure 3.4) and by your bodily sensations, where your emotional reactions and associations reside and are expressed.

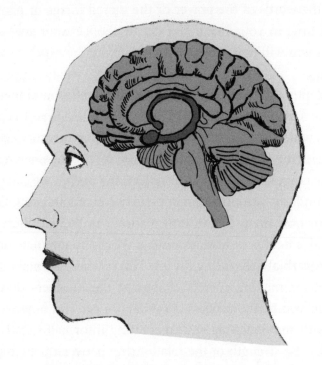

Figure 3.4 The limbic system: regulating your emotions

The brain contains a vast knowledge base of past experiences and the outcomes they once produced. If I make a neurochoice by taking the time to observe my emotions and choose my actions, I can regulate my own mood and create my own happiness. The body also has a memory, which can return us to the experience of prior events. This is valuable information to the observer who is questioning whether those emotions are a match to the present event and using the information for making choices about actions. These bodily memories can also be a nightmare of post-traumatic stress disorder flashbacks; here they take over our consciousness, replaying traumatic events of the past as if they were happening now. Where you choose to focus your attention—and the knowledge you have about what influences you—shapes your expectations, actions, and quality of life. Emotions are information to guide your choices; they are not necessarily reality.

There are many ways of thinking about emotion. Sometimes emotion becomes a defining characteristic for a person who is commonly happy, depressed, or angry. Emotion then becomes an indicator of truth about how things are under certain circumstances or an identifying characteristic of a person. Emotion is also related to our circumstances. Our most painful experiences, such as war, violence, or destruction, bring out some of our most painful emotions, but those same situations often bring out the best in us through kindness, compassion, and a collective effort to care for each other. This level of diversity demonstrates the variability in emotion and helps us see emotion as an indicator of meaning, a source of information, and a reservoir of energy that guides and sustains us if we take the time to reflect, receive the information, and be sustained by the purpose found there.

When emotion is understood as information, then emotional experience can be regulated, enhanced, or extinguished. Sometimes "a good cry" is beneficial. Sometimes it's time to stop crying and move on. These are choices we make daily, regulating the emotions that are felt in the body, observed in the brain, and expressed in behavior. When efforts to shift undesirable emotions do not produce a satisfactory experience, psychology offers numerous ways, in the many and varied types of individual and group psychotherapy, that experience can be changed if emotion is viewed as information for guidance. These choices will be discussed in detail in chapter 7, which focuses on ways to shift your state when the unwanted experience is present. That is the power of thought, reflection, and knowledge of the brain. I can get myself in a pretty depressed mood watching the news, eating and drinking substances that are depressants, dysregulating my sleep, taking on more than I can successfully do, and spending time listening to those who like to complain but do not want to improve. Or I can do the opposite. It's up to me. I know about the neurochoices I have. With the help of this book, you will too.

How Executive Functions Manage Information

As the cingulate sustains your focus on the facts collected in working memory and how it feels when emotion is manifested, your frontal lobe engages other abilities called executive functions. These abilities enable you to organize and prioritize information; reason through the implications to form your conclusions into concepts about the situation, person, or possibility; and plan what you anticipate to be the best outcome. They are called executive functions because they manage all the information passing through the brain. Using your executive functions to choose which skills you will develop into automatic responses is the basis for your ability to activate neuroplasticity and build the neural networks in your brain. The place in the frontal lobes where the executive functions do their conscious work is called working memory because this is the work space where you pull all the information together and from which you move forward in thought and in action. This is the final location where it all comes together in your awareness. It is a very busy place in your head.

EXECUTIVE FUNCTIONS

Goal initiation

Goal maintenance (maintaining a train of thought and action)

Flexibility and resilience

Impulse control or inhibition

Perseveration/control

Analysis

Categorization

Verbal fluency

Reasoning (factual, interpretive, without emotion,
   with emotion)

Sequencing/prioritizing

Planning

Decision making

Anticipation

Resourcefulness/creativity

Working memory integration

Past knowledge

Organization of multicomponent schemes (without emotion,
   with emotion)

Estimating time

Scheduling time

Execution of schedule

Understanding Emotional Information

So, what about this emotional information that we are constantly observing as part of the formula for how we experience the world? Emotions are processed in brain structures located deep in the center of the brain. This is where the limbic system is found, with pathways that bring information up from the body through the spinal cord and on into the cortex. The molecules that conduct emotional information are called neuropeptides. There are large concentrations of neuropeptides in the body around the major organs like the heart. These molecules are the means for experiencing emotion and are the guiding mechanism of your "gut sense."

Neuropsychologist Candace Pert produced the groundbreaking research that identified the location and function of the neuropetides, which are now commonly called the molecules of emotion.[1] As the pathways of interconnection are discovered, we are beginning to understand the enormity of the information coming to the brain from the body. Many of the psychological methods that have been found to be powerful both in healing emotional and psychological pain and in discovering each person's unique "truth" are based in enhancing a consciousness of bodily sensations. Emotions are information about what is or is not good for us. When we focus our attention and use working memory, taking the time to look there and think about what is happening, we can gain awareness of the information that resides in the body.

There are entire areas of clinical methods designed to teach us how to do this. One such method, called focusing, guides people toward an awareness of the bodily sensations that contribute information. Focusing promotes self-examination for better decision making. This method and many more rely on this powerful intelligence manifested by the molecules of emotion in the body.

FOCUSING: A METHOD FOR USING YOUR BODY AS A GUIDE
Focusing is a therapeutic method developed by Eugene Gendlin, PhD, who studied the characteristics of experience as described by clients benefiting from therapy. Gendlin observed the physical sensations that clients reported in response to the change they felt was manifesting. He coined the term "felt sense" to describe the feeling of what was happening, "felt shift" for the change in how a conflict had been experienced as it was resolved, and "experiential listening" for a way of attending to the felt undercurrents of an issue being discussed. This method is based in the body knowledge that guides the focuser to greater and greater accuracy in their insight and reflection. (See the Awakening Applications at the end of the chapter for ways you can benefit from focusing.)

Information Highway of the Autonomic Nervous System

The pathways that carry emotional information back and forth between the brain and the body are largely contained in the autonomic nervous system, which has two distinct branches (see Figure 3.5). The sympathetic branch functions to make us aware of responses to thoughts and experiences that have emotional content. It is sensitive, or sympathetic, to what is happening. The parasympathetic branch reinstates balance and soothes us after emotional activation. Both of these branches are under the control of the awakened brain when you become aware of their

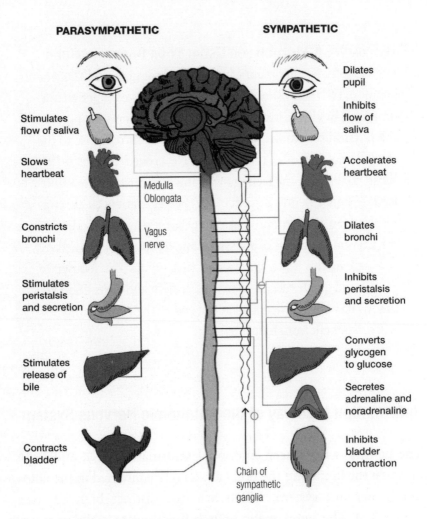

PARASYMPATHETIC

SYMPATHETIC

Dilates
pupil

Stimulates
flow of saliva

Inhibits
flow of
saliva

Slows
heartbeat

Accelerates
heartbeat

Medulla
Oblongata

Constricts
bronchi

Vagus
nerve

Dilates
bronchi

Stimulates
peristalsis
and secretion

Inhibits
peristalsis
and secretion

Converts
glycogen
to glucose

Stimulates
release of
bile

Secretes
adrenaline and
noradrenaline

Contracts
bladder

Inhibits
bladder
contraction

Chain of
sympathetic
ganglia

Figure 3.5 Autonomic Nervous System: regulating sensation and emotion

function and methods for regulation. One of the greatest contribu-
tors to methods of regulation is the field of biofeedback, which
brings the brain and body connection into awareness. In contrast
to this view that emotions are information to assist your choices,

many people consider themselves to be their emotions. Hence, there is the "angry person," "depressed person," or "the joker." Now neuroscience is showing us that emotions are chemicals that are information passed along the highway of the nervous system to be used to help us understand our experience and make our decisions accordingly. That is what neurochoice is all about.

When you understand the autonomic nervous system and use the information it offers for guidance, you have available a powerful feedback system for consciously understanding the individual meaning of events. Something magnificent and awe inspiring, like a first glimpse of the Grand Canyon, the deep peace of a slumbering newborn baby, or the vastness of the stars in the night sky, can automatically produce a deep, expansive feeling where a sense of total safety, richness, and depth emerges from deep within the nervous system. This is the regulation of the parasympathetic nervous system activating a wonderful, fulfilling response to an unforgettable moment. As we learn to read the radar screen of the body and understand the more subtle guidance of the nervous system, we can fine-tune our awareness of what is happening and refine the effectiveness of our choices to actually produce the outcomes we seek in life. This is how the autonomic nervous system expands your consciousness by delivering the information of the feeling.

Brain-Body Compass

Let's go back to our discussion of the frontal lobes as the inter-section where cognitive functions come together and add to the mix the power of the "gut sense" that gives us information for processing a decision or for arriving at an insight in working memory. Over the years of observing my own experience and that of the hundreds of people I have been privileged to work with, I have come to think of this information source as the Brain-Body Compass (see Figure 3.6). Obviously, a compass is a dynamic instrument used to guide us in our travel and assist us in finding our way to a desired destination. There are many other mechanisms for this purpose, such as the radar screen and the GPS. But for the sake of simplicity, let's use the compass as the metaphor for the emotional information coming into consciousness in the brain from the body, which is the needle of the compass. That information can be held in awareness in working memory to enhance the efficacy of our decisions.

The function of a compass is to contribute constantly changing information that will assist us as we move through life experiences, seeking our path to a desired destination. A compass guides us by pointing to "true north" so that we will recognize what course we are on and adapt according to our desired destination. Prior to the compass, the North Star guided travelers as they charted their course and pursued their explorations. So again, for the sake of simplicity, let's say you are "seeking your true north" when you are looking for the best possible outcome for a decision, and think of your body as the compass you must read to reach it.

If emotions are information to the awakened brain, the bodily sensations of those emotions are the needle on the Brain-Body Compass. Think of the needle as pointing to your true north when you encounter the information you need to succeed in a desired outcome; this means that when you hold the information about a possibility in your working memory and imagine arriving at that destination in life, you feel an unequivocal, enthusiastic, positive response from your body. "True north" is hitting the jackpot in a

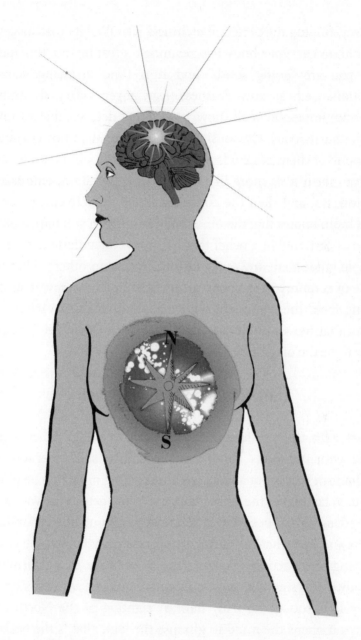

Figure 3.6 The Brain-Body Compass: the brain awake to sensation and emotion

big way, finding the perfect match, and KNOWING that success is assured. When your body is screaming a great big no, this means that you are "going south" and it is time to change course. Emotions such as powerlessness, fear, anger, worry, frustration, and even hopefulness all show, to different degrees, that you have not found the way. Obviously, hope is closer than powerlessness, but none of them are evidence of an emphatic yes. Getting closer to true north feels more like optimism, expectation, enthusiasm, passion, joy, and then the confidence of KNOWING. The awakened brain knows that the inner reality, in which you have a bodily sense of certainty in a belief that has not yet manifested, is a more reliable guide than any outer information from others. That total sense of certainty in the body grounds us in the energy of success. Acting from the alignment with that kind of KNOWING is the power that moves mountains. It is the tiny mustard seed that can grow to be the biggest bush.

Entering the Realm of Belief

I start with this crash course in neuropsychology when clients come with questions about their cognitive skills, because any mechanism that is not adequately functioning must first be understood. What makes the action happen? What gets in the way of the desired action? Once you have concepts about how your brain works and just what is limiting its processing, you have a basis for grasping what action you can take to improve its performance. Usually, understanding these concepts is a necessary first step, but rarely is it enough to truly have a "sighting of the North Star." Rather, it opens the mind to glimpse the logic that is the basis for hope and a map to guide the effort when the motivation is there.

Commonly, patients are more likely to have an emphatic yes to the possibility of recovering from brain injury or training a desired cognitive skill when they meet someone who has successfully faced those same challenges. When people lack the belief that they, too, can achieve their goal, I usually have them talk to someone else who is living proof that the outcome they seek is possible. That is usually the turning point, when the glimmer of hope becomes a real possibility for them, sufficient to make a neurochoice to get up each day and work that muscle of the brain yet again. Then as their skills improve, they, too, have an inner KNOWING that they can achieve the goal they seek. I saw this glimmer in Kathy, the woman I met on the train, when I told her of my success with my health challenges. When she said, "That was what I needed to know," I saw that, for Kathy, my story had enough science and real-life credibility to it that she was enabled to shift her expectations of herself. Neuropsychology provides the concepts and knowledge of how the brain works and what you can do to make it work better. It is entering the realm of belief and having the inner desire become real that sustains the effort every day, which makes the dream become reality. Then something that does not now exist is experienced as a reality that can be created. A certainty or KNOWING emerges.

How do we understand this experience of KNOWING? What is it, how do you get there, and where does it take you? In the past, the certainty of KNOWING has been a characteristic observed in great leaders who spoke with inspiring certainty, the mystics and enlightened whose faith was unshakable because they seemed to "see" something others did not. Leaders, healers, saints, and sages all seem to have it, but what is it?

In the convent, I was exposed to a discernment process. When a big decision had to be made, people were encouraged to take time for this process. This means going through the steps of identifying the many qualities or dimensions of the issue or question; expanding upon what is involved and exploring the implications of the perspective; and finally, praying about the question and expecting to be guided to the answer. All this is done in the context of the principles of a person's beliefs and values. But how does that happen from a neuropsychological perspective?

There are many psychological methods for discernment. Focusing, mentioned earlier in this chapter, is a comprehensive interactive approach: one person speaks while a second person listens. Then the listener repeats what they have just heard, and the speaker then takes time to sense how they feel about what they have said as they're hearing it repeated. This engages the body's wisdom for what feels right and gives the speaker time to consider why it feels right. But in a religious community, the discernment process takes another dimension as well, and that is prayer. This includes an awareness of the sacred dimension of the question and an openness to guidance on this deeper level of KNOWING. Our experiences have many dimensions and depths that are available to be explored but are easily missed. Bringing the sacred dimension to our consciousness changes what we see, broadens and deepens the meaning, and makes available a rich wealth of strength. This is why I often discuss with people in therapy the meaning of what is happening, and reflect back to them their own descriptions so that they can consider what they are telling themselves. They KNOW when they have found the bull's-eye of an issue instead of just hitting the target or the barn. The bull's-eye feels different and leads to a different outcome. It registers in a unique way on the Brain-Body Compass.

Waking up to what is possible means cultivating an awareness of how to manage your brain, emotions, and choices for creating the life you seek. Siddhartha reinvented himself, as have others in history. Some have become spiritually enlightened, found great compassion for others, or developed passions that led to contributions that have changed this world. What is inspiring is that you can invent or reinvent yourself by learning about how your brain works, discovering what you have to work with in your cognitive style, and making your own neurochoice, holding a vision in your mind's eye while living what you know is possible.

Awakening Applications

- Belief is at the heart of your ability to expand your brain's function and achieve what you really want out of life. To assess your own level of belief, ask yourself some key questions and be honest with the answers: Do you think your brain is capable of sustaining a focus? Do you think you would succeed if you tried to achieve a goal? If you answered yes to these questions, you have a strong level of belief that will serve you in living your goals. If you answered no, then it is helpful to get in touch with your "felt sense." By answering no, you probably had the sensation of hitting a wall. So start by asking yourself what you need in order to be successful in achieving your goal. Try on different answers. Your felt sense will light up when you find the answer you need. Trusting that sensation gives you the belief you need to succeed.

- Your emotions are information for you to use in guiding your neurochoices. Start to see your emotions as an indicator of meaning and a reservoir of energy that can guide and sustain you. Instead of letting them sweep you away, take the time to reflect on your emotions, receive the valuable information contained in them, and let the purpose found in them lead you to the answers you seek.

- Your brain's cingulate regulates your emotions. The stronger your cingulate, the more control you have over your experience. With control, you are able to guide your experiences to the outcomes you desire. The good news is that you have the power to strengthen your cingulate, and one way is through breath work. It can be as simple as quietly attending to breathing deeply into your lower diaphragm to the count of three and slowly breathing out to the count of five, allowing all your muscles to release and your emotions to mellow on the out breath. This combination soothes your nerves, quiets the chatter of your mind, and expands the strength of your focus.

- Focusing is a method that helps you become more aware of your bodily sensations, which gives you valuable information that can guide your decisions. It's your tool for reading your Brain-Body Compass. Here's a way to incorporate the general principle into your own life: The next time you are faced with a decision, test out different options and notice how your body responds. Do you feel tense? Does your breathing become shallow or constricted? Once the issue has been resolved, do you feel a shift in your body's sensations? Do you then feel your shoulders relax and a certain lightness to your body? By paying attention to the physical effects of your emotions and decisions, you can begin to listen to your body's wisdom and apply it to your choices.

- By the same token, your Brain-Body Compass lets you know through physical and emotional sensations when you've made a choice that's right for you. When an issue has been resolved favorably for you, take note of what it feels like in your spirit, mind, and body. Get to know that sensation, because it is your "true north." Follow your body's guidance when you are making decisions and observe the results. In time, you will easily recognize your true north and know with certainty that you are on the right track.

Note

1. Candace Pert, *Molecules of Emotion* (New York: Simon & Schuster, 1999).

4

How Emotion as Information
Directs Focus and Energy

M aria was a beautiful, articulate, intelligent little girl. She enjoyed going to school, had lots of friends, and got along well at home. So why had her parents brought her to my office for a neuropsychological evaluation? Although so many things were going well, Maria had some unusual experiences. At story time, when the children were sitting quietly, listening to the book being read to them, Maria participated easily until the scary part came along. At that point she had a tendency to bolt out of the room, unaware of where she was going or why. What was going on? What was causing this unusual behavior?

Maria's parents were highly educated people and wanted information about their child to understand how to best support and guide her. The school psychologist was likewise puzzled by this one striking inconsistency. Maria could not explain it either. All she knew was that she had to get out of the room sometimes and her body just went, leaving her out in the hallway with her heart racing.

The cause of the unusual behavior was that Maria had a very sensitive autonomic nervous system. This reaction was triggered when she was startled or scared, and no amount of intelligence or focus was available to her as she went flying out the door. On a physiological level, this is called the "stress response" or the activation of the hypothalamic pituitary adrenal axis (HPAA) (see Figure 4.1). Maria was very sensitive in this way, and had no control over her body when she was frightened and this part of her nervous system took over. Her arms and legs just got going and took her out of wherever she was, even during story time.

WHAT HAPPENS IN A STRESS RESPONSE

- The stress response activates the hypothalamic pituitary adrenal axis (HPAA).
- The hypothalamus releases corticotrophine release factor (CRF).
- CRF engages the pituitary gland and activates the release of adrenocorticotropic hormones (ACTH).
- ACTH directs the adrenal glands to release adrenaline into the body.
- Adrenal glands activate stress hormones and functions for the fight-or-flight response.
- The immune system is suppressed.
- Blood vessels constrict in the digestive system.
- Blood is forced to the arms, legs, heart, and brain.
- The brain goes into hypervigilance and defensive mode and no longer sees the big picture.

To learn more about how the stress response happens in your body, I recommend reading *The Biology of Belief* by Bruce Lipton.[1]

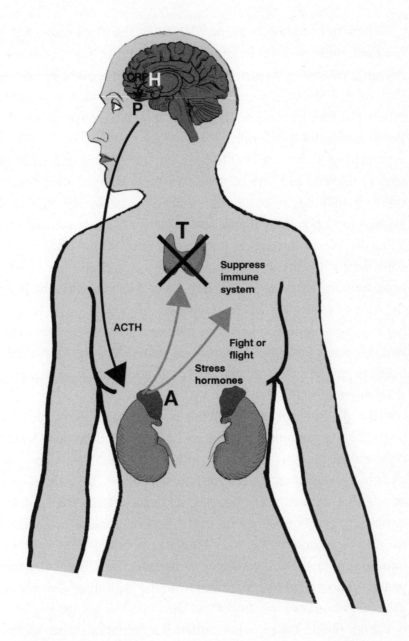

Figure 4.1 HPAA: hypothalamic pituitary adrenal axis for the fight-or-flight response

Thankfully, today we know a lot about the physiology of this reaction, most commonly known as the fight-or-flight response. As you'll see in this chapter, it is very possible to regulate responses that we feel in our bodies as a result of our autonomic nervous system. In fact, learning to be in charge of these responses is the key to awakening your brain.

I explained this reaction to Maria in a way she could relate to and, at six years old, she started learning to recognize the sensations developing in her body prior to a stress response and learned to stop and breathe as soon as she was aware of what was going on. We discussed how her heart would race but if she would consistently breathe in and out, her lungs would give her heart a nice, soothing massage to slow it down and help it relax. She liked the idea of giving her heart a massage; she said it was a lot like petting the cat. She also knew she felt much better when her heart was not racing and when her muscles weren't tensing. Maria liked being happy, so she breathed deeply and took charge of changing what did not feel good to her.

In explaining specific mechanisms of the autonomic nervous system, I use examples of children I have treated because young children respond to treatment without thought or without an already-developed rationale. Adults, in contrast, have developed minds that automatically provide an explanation, often quickly attributing events to someone in the past or present. In children we see the autonomic nervous system responding while they ask questions after the fact to discover meaning. This is the simplest picture of how all of us progressed from the beginning of our lives: the brain observes experiences and then puts names and explanations on them. When adults offer interpretations and soothe emotions, young brains begin to develop an interpretation for their perceptions. The power of those explanations and soothing either enhances brain function or limits it. Adults also have the same type of reactions but are usually focused on the outer events, not the inner events we are focusing on here.

Making Sense of Our Experience

Maria provided a beautiful illustration of how children discover their own meaning through after-the-fact questioning. As we discussed how well she was doing in regulating her body and creating her experience the way she liked it, Maria said she had a question she had been thinking about. She wanted to know what kind of a girl she was. The question surprised me, so I asked her what she meant. "Well, I'm not a girly girl or a tomboy, so who am I?" At a very young age, Maria was becoming aware of herself and others, and her brain searched for an interpretation of her experience to create the meaning that felt right.

We both agreed that the answer would come with time and more life experience. But for now, we knew from the testing that she was smart and had strong academic skills, and she was obviously pretty and very nice to others. She seemed satisfied to leave the answer at "smart, pretty, and nice girl," which felt good to her. Even her young mind was creating meaning.

The concept of developing "coherence of mind," a phrase Dr. Dan Siegel uses in his book *The Mindful Brain*, is a helpful description of Maria's experience. We all attempt to reconcile ambiguous or contradictory information to create a coherent understanding of events.[2] We especially benefit from such reconciliation in the observations of ourselves. Maria was trying to make sense of her experiences to create a meaningful image of herself. This is what the brain does. It is programmed to make sense of our experiences.

What about boys? Similar questions come from them. One little guy who preferred to play with girls also came to my office because, again, his parents were trying to understand how to make sense of his experience and answer his questions. Ben was unusually intelligent and highly intuitive. For example, he could precisely describe the soothing feeling of the amethyst bookends on the windowsill in contrast to the feeling of the exciting crystal on the desk.

Ben also had an experience of finding himself running out of the room. For him, it was running out of the gym when the other boys were extremely active and completely overloading him with more stimulation than his nervous system could handle. On the day of this event, he also asked a question, seeking coherence in his experience. "Am I a girl in a boy's body?" he asked his teacher as his heart raced and he struggled to get control of himself.

Ben preferred to play with girls because they were nicer, talked to him, and listened to what he had to say. From Ben's test results, this made perfect sense; young boys are typically delayed in language development compared to girls, but Ben was very advanced for his age. He won prizes for coming up with words and could explain himself in a very sophisticated way.

In both Ben's and Marie's cases, it was instructive to watch the children formulate their questions and see their little bodies relax into an answer that satisfied them. They did not need to know about the chemistry of the HPAA and the fight-or-flight response. It was enough for them to know about what was scary and too much versus what was fun and just right. They could easily imagine something they enjoyed or something that frightened them and convey the feeling in their bodies when they had those thoughts. With a little practice, even a six-year-old can enjoy a heart massage by pacing the breath and returning to a harmonious physical state. As adults, we have an even greater capacity to observe and question our reaction to situations, read the meaning in our behaviors, and relax into answers that satisfy us as we continue to expand our brains.

Reading Emotional Information in Order to Know Your Glass Ceiling

One of the brain structures that is instrumental in the regulation of emotion and physical sensation is the insula, a part of the cortex where an awareness of bodily emotional states is located. It is positioned in the cortex to integrate information about the sensations in the body (called somatic markers) that indicate emotional meaning.[3] This is where the feeling of what is happening comes into awareness and can be used as information to guide behavior. Reflecting on how a person, situation, or opportunity feels to you is essential information in decision making. Using the emotional awareness from the insula is part of a very conscious and deliberate system in the brain that provides valuable information for insight. It, too, is part of the limbic system that processes emotion, but it works in a very different way than the stress response, which is hardwired to protect us in emergencies. The insula appears to be a significant part of the brain's ability to use emotional information in thinking.

The distinction between integrating emotional information in a way that is reactive—automatic or reflective—and food for thought makes all the difference in your ability to regulate your nervous system rather than be controlled by it. One way to put your insula to work and read the emotional information coming to you is to pay attention to the mechanisms of your own nervous system, depicted in the following figure, and to learn to regulate them.

Figure 4.2 is an illustration of some of the characteristics now understood to be part of the regulation of the autonomic nervous system. Research suggests that different levels or types of arousal in the nervous system create behavioral outcomes, which explains the behaviors of Ben and Maria.[4] I tell my patients that they have to pay attention to the glass ceiling that indicates the limits of their well-being. On a good day, when you've had plenty of rest and things are going well, you can tolerate a lot more stress and still manage your emotions. That is a day when the glass ceiling is high, giving you lots of wiggle room to be active. On a bad day, when you are tired or already emotionally overloaded, it does not take much stress to activate negative emotion and reactivate physical symptoms like headaches. With practice, you will be able to observe yourself over time and recognize the warning signs of fatigue and irritability that indicate trouble is coming. Being able to recognize the emotional and physical indicators of a fluctuating nervous system is the beginning of being awake to making neurochoices for a harmonious life.

In Figure 4.2, the Optimal Arousal Zone indicates the range of activity and rest that produces just the right amount of stimulation you need to maximize your skills and abilities. The Moving Glass Ceiling is the indicator of the current range of tolerance of your nervous system, which is ever-changing. The Hyperarousal Zone is the territory where you get too much stimulation and you freak out, lose it, and sometimes become your worst self. Thanks to neuroscience, it is now understood that each of these states is regulated by a different part of the nervous system and activated by chemical communication.

Autonomic Nervous System Regulation

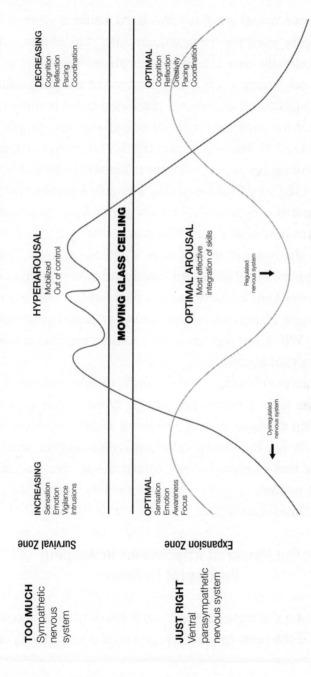

Figure 4.2 The moving glass ceiling: autonomic nervous system regulation[5]

The hyperarousal state is considered to be a survival state, intended to be used for "emergencies only." The ability to think broadly, creatively, and intelligently is absent when the sympathetic nervous system takes over. This type of arousal produces a state that is grounded in fear and reactivity, and it literally makes you stupid. After experiencing such an arousal state, people often ask themselves, "What was I thinking?" The answer is that you weren't thinking, because you couldn't. You were hijacked by your amygdala, the part of the brain that sets off an emergency alarm and activates the fight-or-flight response, which causes you to lose access to perspective and reflection.

It is in the optimal arousal state where we are our smartest, nicest, and most effective, coordinated, and aware. I like to call it the Expansion Zone because this is where I see growth and excellence available. Here is where you find your skills—your basis for expansion. When you regulate your emotion, you get on the path to accessing your best self.

As we develop language and scientific insight into ourselves in this way, we have a means for making sense of our senses and words to think about our experiences, which produces better judgment. When the frontal lobe can reflect and the left hemisphere can find symbols, words, and concepts to represent our experience to communicate, you have available to you the power of focused, intentional living.

The Power of Attachment in Shaping the Neural Network

Young children want to explore and discover their fascinating world, but at the same time they seek a secure base in the parental relationship. They rely on the parental relationship for the protection they are not yet able to supply themselves and as a means of learning interpretations and ways of coping with emotions and challenges.[6] When a child experiences a parent's delight in response to their actions, there is a shared joy in the healthy aspects of life. It is in the sharing of this state that behaviors become more automatic and neural networks are reinforced. When a child encounters frightening, threatening, and confusing events, he or she turns to the parent for a secure base. The parent is then able to both provide safety and help organize and articulate the confusing experience that the child has encountered but does not understand. Because the child can turn to the parent for successful assistance, the parent is teaching the child that Mom/Dad is reliable, as well as showing the child how to cope with and understand emotions, events, and behavior. New neural pathways are constantly forming in response to every new experience. Repetitive experience strengthens associations that later become automatic.

Psychology describes the effect of the environment and relationships in early childhood in terms of the type of attachments that are formed, and it turns out that these attachments affect the wiring of the young brain.[7] A secure attachment is formed in a relationship where the child is consistently safe, assisted, respected, and loved. A disorganized or disoriented attachment is one where inconsistencies abound. Parents who say they spank a child because they love the child are giving a very confusing message about the meaning of love in relationships, and these feeling states are hardwired with repeated experience. Such emotional and behavioral inconsistency can result in an emotional dysregulation and dysfunction for the child in adult relationships later in life.

The opposite is also true. Consistent, safe, stable, and loving relationships with parents, teachers, coaches, or therapists can effectively establish a basis for healthy relationships even when past trauma has had an effect. When a child feels loved by another person, receives explanations and solutions, and subsequently achieves beneficial outcomes, a new effect manifests in the nervous system.

"Human beings of all ages are found to be their happiest and to be able to deploy their talents to best advantage when they are confident that, standing behind them, there are one or more trusted persons who will come to their aid should difficulty arise."[8] These are the words of John Bowlby, a British psychologist who wrote extensively on attachment and separation in development. He captures beautifully the change in the nervous system that is felt immediately and physically when we know ourselves to be grounded in secure, productive relationships.

Fortunately for Billy, another child who came to my office for treatment, his dad was just such an influence in his life. Billy's father was concerned that his son lacked the character of good sportsmanship. Billy was a football player who, at times, got out of control. One such incident resulted in Billy injuring another player after the play had ended. This was long before the current growing awareness of the prevalence of concussions in contact sports. A blow to the head can result in a concussion and can also unleash emotions and uncharacteristic behavior.

At some point during the game, Billy sustained a concussion in the rough activity. Later, when another player forcefully shoved and knocked him to the ground, Billy suddenly rose to his feet and attacked the other boy, injuring him severely. This was a puzzle to the coach, Billy's dad, and especially Billy, who had never experienced anything like it before. What happened? Billy was hijacked by his amygdala, the activator of the fight-or-flight response. Unfortunately, Billy was oriented to fight rather than flight, and the other player got hurt. Billy lashed out and afterward had no idea why. When this lashing out happens with traumatic brain injury, the diagnosis for aggressive, uncontrollable behavior is called combative and requires restraints.

Because he struggled with controlling his emotions, it became clear that the intense stimulation of football was not for Billy. But fortunately he made progress because his dad offered him a better option. They took up golf and played regularly together. It was a special time for Billy to be with his dad, who worked long hours and often was not home. Golfing was not competitive for them. Golf was the only time Billy had his dad all to himself. As they both learned to play, Billy's skill surpassed that of his dad, who enjoyed and encouraged Billy's success. Over time Billy was able to play competitively under stress without experiencing the pattern of reactivity that had become so habitual and disabling for him. With the stabilizing influence of his father's steady emotions and behavior, Billy dismantled a neural network of automatic reactivity that had controlled him.

Likewise, first grader Maria is learning to control her heart rate and recognize the meaning of sensations in her body. As she grows up, her awareness of her emotions and the information they provide will offer her insights and choices that few children have at such an early age.

Ben's parents were concerned about his sensitivity, personality development, and gender identification, but they found out that their son has verbal skills at the 99th percentile. Because Ben possesses such extraordinary verbal talent, he enjoys reading and talking far more than the rough and tumble activities of other boys his age. With that perspective, they consider how to best assist him in developing these talents and understanding his relationships with other boys and girls who are similar to or different from him.

Billy's unsportsmanlike behavior was actually produced by an undetected concussion, which disinhibited his emotions and unleashed an automatic protective response in his nervous system, which was beginning to shape his personality. His brain sought coherence, interpreting his emotions and behavior to create meaning. At the time he came for testing, he was beginning to think of aggressive behavior as an advantage in winning at sports, which he viewed as the ultimate goal. His relationship with his father turned around a tendency to become a bully and helped him dismantle the automatic aggressive reaction he had been cultivating. Over time he learned to enjoy and take pride in the athletic talents he possessed and took satisfaction in perfecting his skill with a cool head.

Parents who promote their children's development by having them focus on the guidance within them, and who participate with their children in the exploration of the meaning of experience, are opening the doors for the development of an awakened brain. From this perspective, parents open doors of possibility that children can enter when they are ready. By observing children, you are also gaining insight into yourself in both the present and the past. Your parents influenced the emotional and behavioral habits you learned. Just like Maria, Ben, and Billy, we all try to make sense of our experiences in order to have a coherent mind. When we take the time to do so, we make neurochoices that lead us to our Optimal Arousal Zone, where better outcomes and further expansion await us.

The Meaning of Emotions

In my experience, most people believe their emotions are reality. When someone says, "I'll tell you the truth," it usually means "This is really how I feel when _____, and the experience is so strongly embodied in my body sensations that I believe this to be the reality." When this is the case, sensation and emotion are the conductors of the orchestra and they determine the tune for generating your behavior. The brain is good at coming up with explanations of why it is advantageous to be a bully or why boys are scary and girls are nice. Making up explanations is what the brain does.

Thankfully, neuroscience has given us lots of new perspectives on ourselves. Just because Maria's heart is racing doesn't mean she must leave the room. Over time she can learn to think about her sensations and emotions rather than be them. With repeated practice in observing how she feels, Maria can recognize when situations are good for her in contrast to those that are too much, rather than reacting and creating trouble for herself. With time and repeated practice, emotions become information that guides the focus of attention and directs the energy of action. Parents who are aware of this, and who discuss their own feelings for the creation of meaning, model an awareness of their inner world. Children of these parents are way ahead of the game.

Neuroscience is likewise showing us the benefit of these efforts to observe emotions for grasping meaning. It turns out that the number of fibers that go from the limbic system to the cortex to regulate thinking and behavior are running the show in childhood. The number of limbic fibers going up into the cortex significantly outnumbers the number of fibers going from the cortex to the limbic system, where thoughts and emotional responses are regulated (see Figure 4.3). Hence, emotions trigger responses of laughing, crying, throwing, and grabbing. The good news is that, with time and practice, the reverse develops. As adults we no longer scream, throw things, or cry when we are uncomfortable, as we did in childhood. The intensity of emotion is dampened by our ability to reflect, develop language and concepts, and recall past solutions, which puts thought and choice in charge of emotion and behavior.

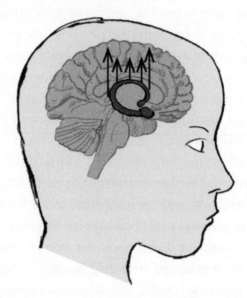

Figure 4.3 Cortical: limbic fibers of a child's brain—emotion determines behavior

When the number of fibers coming down from the cortex to the limbic system outnumbers those going from the limbic system to the cortex (as in Figure 4.4), the power of neurochoice is available. The executive operating officer can now focus on the Brain-Body Compass, read the sensations, and choose the action for the desired outcome rather than express raw emotion. When

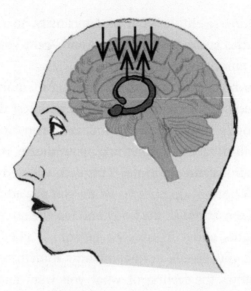

Figure 4.4 Cortical: limbic fibers of an adult's brain—emotion is monitored by thought

you can consider the facts in working memory and anticipate which response will result in the desired outcome, you are awake to what you are doing.

We have often heard that home is where the heart is. In that same perspective, reality is where the focus is. To create your life deliberately, you need to have the capacity to use the cingulate and working memory to process emotion as information, and then use that information to direct thought and action. All it takes is training yourself to observe your habits of what you pay attention to, how you feel, and the sense of your identity that emerges in that state. When learning to read the language of emotional information, you must learn to decode the smaller signals of sensation, which are the mood's message, in order to comprehend the meaning. You feel those sensations as emotional shifts, like sadness, enthusiasm, and curiosity, to name a few. Take note of the emotion's sensation, and soon you will easily recognize the emotion's meaning.

When you hold an intention in working memory and focus on the unfolding of the steps necessary to manifest the outcome, your Brain-Body Compass guides you each step along the way. When you think about something you desire, the thought activates sensations and emotions. This is considered to be a top-down effect. A bottom-up effect is when you pay attention to the emotions and sensations in the body and use the interpretation to develop thoughts about a topic or person. It goes both ways. When you use your insula to imagine how something might feel, your body knows the feeling of what you want and will know when you get there.

All these are reactions and awareness you can train in yourself. You get to decide where you will come from within yourself. You can "choose the eyes you will see with" by determining what you want to look for. You can see the best or worst in someone. It is up to you. Just like we decide which hat to wear today, which signifies choosing among the many roles we play, the intention you hold in your mind and focus on throughout the day will determine your outcome.

The "eyes of expectancy" represent a specific mind-set. We find what we expect to see. One experience triggers the next. Once an intention is set in the brain, it is like setting the dial on a detector for the alarm to sound in the presence of your interest. The compass of your body recognizes the sensation and guides you forward. For some this is easy and natural. For others it is a learned skill. Each brain is unique, but we all have emotion and can learn to recognize the presence of different emotions and their meaning.

The Optimal Arousal State Represents an Expansion Zone

In Figure 4.2, the optimal arousal state indicates the amount of stimulation that is "just right."[9] Like in the children's story "Goldilocks and the Three Bears," where Goldilocks finds one porridge that is too hot, one that is too cold, and one that is just right, the fine-tuning of emotion perfects our experience like temperature perfected her breakfast. As I mentioned earlier in the chapter, the optimal arousal state is where you can access your broadest range of skills and the most precise, effective, and timely use of your abilities in awareness, focus, sensation, pacing, and coordination. This is where your best self is found.

It is within the optimal arousal state that the ventral parasympathetic nervous system produces a feeling of harmony, coherence, and alignment. This is the state to come from to reflect, adapt, be constructive, and be productive. This is where the "rest and digest" response is accessed to promote physical wellness and where you can find the emotions that make you smart. Secure attachment is also fostered here, which makes you feel like a smart winner in life. Relationships fostered from the optimal arousal state produce the sense of belonging that brings forth the best self.

When I reflect on my own life and my observations of the people I have worked with in my career, this information about the mechanisms of regulating optimal arousal in the nervous system seems to be at the heart of success for us all. It matters not if you are an athlete, parent, politician, teacher, or pilot; anyone interested in developing their abilities and achieving greater success is learning to regulate his or her nervous system to achieve expansion. The basis for all achievement is the knowledge of where the target is located, what the bull's-eye looks like, and how to get there. This is your neuropsychological treasure map.

The Extinction Zone:
When the Automatic Nervous System Shuts You Down

If we do so well regulating the amount of stimulation in the nervous system to the optimal range, why would we ever come out of this state? Good question! There are a lot of reasons why people engage in hyperarousal states. Sometimes life events, such as a tragedy on the scale of 9/11 or natural disasters like earthquakes and tsunamis, cause all of us to be flooded with adrenaline. These are true emergencies, and they are the reason that we have a survival mechanism in the nervous system to keep us safe and alive. But sometimes people just like the thrill of the adrenaline rush and consider it entertainment. The excitements of movies, amusement parks, technology war games, sports events, and gambling all produce the thrill of an adrenaline rush.

Now, there is nothing wrong with some excitement and fun, which is different from fear. The hyperarousal state was designed for emergency use only. When it is consistently operative over time, the chemical effects literally shut down your digestive system, your immune system, and the creative parts of your brain. An emergency mechanism is for exactly that—an emergency. Under those conditions, you are hyperfocused on the immediate threat, and blood flow goes primarily to your legs and arms to protect you. It is designed for short-term use only and has detrimental effects on your well-being when used extensively.

We have talked about the glass ceiling—when too much arousal makes you out of control and stupid—but what about the glass floor? What is happening for people who become the "deer in headlights"? There are those times when there is too little arousal and "brain freeze" sets in. This is the sense of being so overloaded or disconnected that no thoughts come and no action is possible. The current theory suggests that this is a state in which the dorsal parasympathetic nervous system is taking over. The level of arousal drops below the glass floor, and you are shut out of the game.

Figure 4.5 depicts an Extinction Zone, where hypoarousal stops the processing of the nervous system. When experiencing the hypoarousal state, you become immobilized and detached. In more severe cases, people dissociate and may lose consciousness. We commonly see this phenomenon in animals in the wild. When the lion is chasing the gazelle, a hyperarousal is triggered so that the gazelle can quickly flee. However, if the lion is fast enough to catch the gazelle, then the hypoarousal system shuts down the nervous system, and the only one suffering is you watching the movie. The gazelle dissociates from the situation and loses consciousness. Hence, another kindness from nature: another emergency system to protect you.

Hypoarousal is a mechanism that protects us from overload. The latest popular terminology for our experience with hypoarousal is brain freeze. When you are bombarded with too much information and too much emotion for too long, the brain starts to shut down to protect you. My patients who experience hypoarousal report increasing numbness, lethargy, blocking of thoughts, and lack of awareness. At the same time sensations, emotions, cognition, reflections, pacing, and motor coordination are also decreasing. At times, patients report standing in the street, unable to move, think, speak, or act on their own behalf in any way. This is

Neuroscience Reveals the Mechanisms of Too Much and Too Little for Autonomic Nervous System Regulation

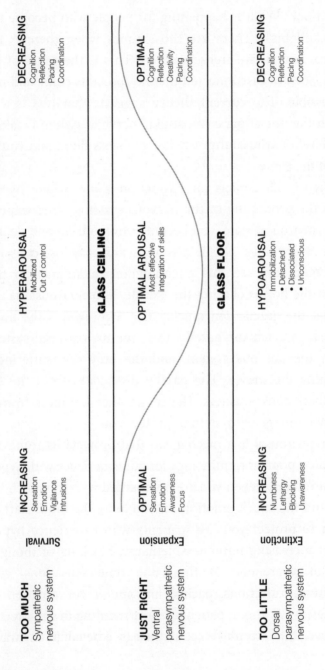

TOO MUCH
Sympathetic nervous system

Survival

INCREASING
Sensation
Emotion
Vigilance
Intrusions

HYPERAROUSAL
Mobilized
Out of control

DECREASING
Cognition
Reflection
Pacing
Coordination

GLASS CEILING

JUST RIGHT
Ventral parasympathetic nervous system

Expansion

OPTIMAL
Sensation
Emotion
Awareness
Focus

OPTIMAL AROUSAL
Most effective integration of skills

OPTIMAL
Cognition
Reflection
Creativity
Pacing
Coordination

GLASS FLOOR

TOO LITTLE
Dorsal parasympathetic nervous system

Extinction

INCREASING
Numbness
Lethargy
Blocking
Unawareness

HYPOAROUSAL
Immobilization
• Detached
• Dissociated
• Unconscious

DECREASING
Cognition
Reflection
Pacing
Coordination

Figure 4.5 Neuroscience reveals the mechanisms of too much and too little for autonomic nervous system regulation.[10]

128

why I call it the Extinction Zone. When you flip this switch in your nervous system, you are shutting down the operation.

Let's look back at the hyperarousal state and see what happens to skills and abilities there. Figure 4.5 shows us that when the sympathetic nervous system takes over, you experience an increase in sensation, emotion, vigilance, and intrusive thoughts. At the same time cognition, reflection, pacing, and coordination decrease. **The autonomic nervous system is creating a state within you that literally alters your access to yourself.**

Often a combination of hyperarousal and hypoarousal occurs in a cycle. Too much arousal floods the nervous system and sets off the alarms, which is not good for your partner or your kids. But staying in that state for very long is exhausting, and a drop into hypoarousal can easily follow (see Figure 4.6). Often a pattern that occurs is that a day in bed is required because things are just too much. In either case, cognition is altered and mistakes are most frequently made in either of these states. They both alter your access to your good intelligence and leave you asking, "What was I thinking?"

When the brain is awake to the meaning of these sensations, you can make neurochoices to manage the nervous system and regulate arousal. This is why the treatment model I use includes stress management with psychotherapy so that people can learn about the fluctuations in their arousal, recognize the sensations that indicate trouble, and know the neurochoices that will get them where they want to go.

Looking back, I recall myself having a hypoarousal response to stress when I was young. I would always get quiet and pull back socially, trying to get perspective on what was happening. This was the opposite of my mother and siblings, who could all talk at once

Consciously Calming the Autonomic Nervous System

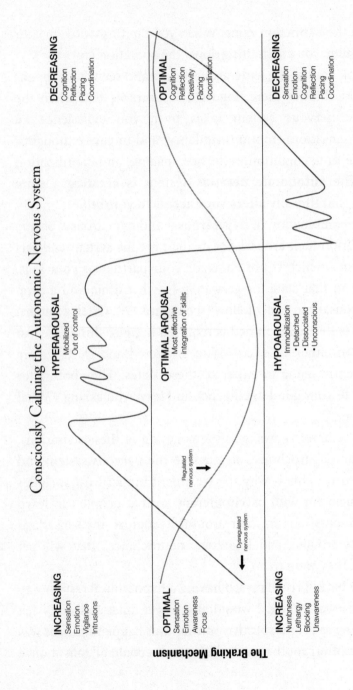

Figure 4.6 Consciously calming the autonomic nervous system.[11]

and somehow seem to hear each other. When I moved to New York City after leaving the convent, I found the high level of activity both exhilarating and overwhelming. But I was determined to learn how the world worked and be able to function in it.

In the '70s I attended a seminar called Erhard Seminars Training, or EST. The intention of the course was to achieve personal growth and enhanced ability to function. It was there that I learned how to get angry. Following years of structured parochial education and then consistent silence in the convent, expressing anger was not in my range of experience. The exercise that stands out in my memory was going on stage as a group in front of a large audience and, with great emphasis, declaring, "Don't you ever, ever, ever brush that dog's teeth with my toothbrush again!" You had to do it with gusto before you could leave the stage.

Once I learned how to get angry, I was much better able to move from hypoarousal into hyperarousal and cope with the intensity of New York City. That experience somehow enabled me to be assertive and push back when I needed to instead of being shut out of the game. I was born in South Dakota, grew up in the suburbs of Michigan, and had entered the convent starting with two years of silence. None of that prepared me for New York, which at times became so overwhelming that it was depressing. Learning to get angry is a perfect antidote for depression. I had to learn how to focus on what I did not want, feel the reactive feelings and the determination to move forward, and then know what to say or do. It has been a great gift to me now that I know how to use it. But at times it got the better of me, and getting out of the hyperarousal state once I was in it was then a new challenge.

After I took the EST course, I attended a ten-day team-building course for health professionals where we completed ropes courses and extreme activities. This was my first experience on a Tyrolean traverse, rappelling off the side of a cliff, and going down a zip line, all of which were stretches for me. I will never forget waiting in line to step off a platform high up in a tree, where there was a cable attached to another tree in the distance on the other side of a valley. As the person in front of me stepped off and flew down the valley, I watched with riveted attention. To my chagrin, something happened at the bottom and he was injured on the landing. Being the next person to step off, I was told to wait where I was, high up on the perch. This was thirty years ago, and I did not know about the autonomic nervous system then; I did know I wanted to keep calm. For an hour, I stood there, waiting. These are the moments when your imagination often becomes worse than reality. As I watched help coming and eventually saw him moving away from the bottom of the cable with assistance, spurts of adrenaline spiked inside of me. I breathed, looked out over the tops of the trees, breathed, thought good thoughts, breathed. Somehow, with each anxiety spike, I turned away and found something else to focus on and returned myself to the positive reason I was standing on that ledge. Over that hour, I managed to keep my focus and keep my cool, calling on every bit of strength within and without. The ride down the zip line was fabulous. The hour standing on the perch was a stretch I will never forget. If I could do it then, I can keep doing it now.

That experience on the zip line is one that I often return to when the world is challenging and I am heading toward hyperarousal. Remembering the feeling of stability in a challenging situation, moving my focus away from the worry when my body is reacting, and focusing on what I want in a situation—this has repeated itself countless times in my life, and it is a response that you can learn as well.

Being aware of your glass ceiling, your Optimal Arousal Zone, and the emotional information that can send you into hyperarousal or hypoarousal are the first steps for successfully regulating your autonomic nervous system. In the next chapter we will move into applying that information in practical ways. Knowing how to breathe, shift your focus, and think about what you want instead of what you don't want is a neurochoice that changes everything.

Awakening Applications

• What's your glass ceiling? Being able to recognize the emotional and physical indicators of your fluctuating nervous system will help you make good decisions every day. Some people hit their glass ceiling if they go too long without eating, without time to be alone, or without time to get off their feet for a while. To get in touch with your glass ceiling, observe when tension starts to build up inside of you. What is going on that leads to this? Observe your emotions and under what circumstances you feel yourself going into hyperarousal. That way you will better understand your fluctuating glass ceiling and what you need to do to stay in optimal arousal. Learn your limitations and give yourself permission to follow the guidance your emotions are giving you. Move away from getting too tired, too angry, too thirsty, or too hungry.

• The cingulate and working memory are valuable tools for processing emotion as information to guide your life choices. In order to put them to use, all it takes is training yourself to observe your habits of what you pay attention to, how you feel, and the sense of your identity that emerges in that state. Under what conditions are you confident and feeling worthy? When are you unsure and vulnerable? What does it mean to you when you observe these experiences? Do you make efforts to change the state you are in to better engage in the experience? Do you focus on the solutions or the problem?

Notes

1. Bruce Lipton, *The Biology of Belief* (Carlsbad, CA: Hay House, 2008).

2. Dan Siegel, *The Mindful Brain* (New York: Norton, 2007), 193.

3. Antonio Damasio, *The Feeling of What Happens* (New York: Harcourt Brace, 1999).

4. Pat Ogden, Kekuni Minton, and Clare Pain, *Trauma and the Body* (New York: Norton, 2006), 32.

5. Ibid.

6. Dan Siegel, *The Developing Mind* (New York: Guilford, 1999).

7. Mary Ainsworth et al., *Patterns of Attachment* (Hillsdale, NJ: Erlbaum, 1978).

8. John Bowlby, *A Secure Base: Clinical Applications of Attachment Theory* (London: Routledge, 1988).

9. Allan Schore, "Right Brain Affect Regulation," *The Healing Power of Emotion*, ed. D. Fosha, J. Siegel, M. Solomon (New York: Norton, 2009), 112–44.

10. Porges, *Polyvagal Theory* (New York: Norton, 2011); Ogden, Minton, and Pain, *Trauma and the Body*, 27.

11. Schore, "Right Brain Affect Regulation," 121.

5

Regulating Emotion: Too Much, Too Little, Just Right

Now that you have seen how the autonomic nervous system causes physical responses in your body, sending you into hyper- or hypoarousal, you are ready to learn how to apply the concepts to regulating your own autonomic nervous system and to be inspired by stories from my clients and from my own life about how this looks in practice. With this knowledge, you can stay in your Optimal Arousal Zone, where your best self is found, and know how to return to it when you find yourself reacting.

The Key to Regulating the Autonomic Nervous System: Managing Your Glass Ceiling

The idea of the glass ceiling came to me during the early days of my career, when there was limited neuroscience, insight into brain function, or language to describe these concepts. Basic concepts like how cognition decreases as emotion goes up were easy for my patients to understand. The concept of fight-or-flight has been around since before I was born, but the understanding of the specific mechanisms and chemistry is still expanding. Even today lots of people do not understand this about themselves. The "glass ceiling" struck me as an appropriate phrase because it was being used at the time to describe a limit that existed in corporate and government leadership, which no one declared but everyone saw. Women were just not getting the executive jobs and higher salaries and did not pass a certain level of advancement in leadership— they were hitting a glass ceiling. The concept fit perfectly with the invisible point in my patients where their limitations started surfacing and changing their emotions, cognition, and behavior.

One striking example of hitting the glass ceiling is the story of a young woman who was injured in a motor vehicle crash. Sharon was just finishing high school and looking forward to college. All those plans disappeared in an instant when an ambulance without a siren went through the red light at the intersection she was approaching. Although she survived the injury and was making her way through rehabilitation, her thinking about the future had not really changed. She had a right hemisphere injury that made it hard for her to take in new information and form new expectations. She also wanted to embrace this new life in college she had so been looking forward to.

I had told her about the glass ceiling and stressed the importance of pacing herself and getting rest between activities during her recovery, but these are foreign concepts to a young person. Yes, yes, yes was the answer she gave me, but the reality was somewhat different. Some lessons must be learned the hard way.

When the day came that Sharon was cleared to go back to her part-time job in a women's apparel store, she was ecstatic. She went back to work, delighted to see her boss and coworkers. She had a flair for selecting the right colors and styles to create a fashionable look, and the customers had missed her assistance. The excitement was so great and the welcome so strong that Sharon forgot everything we had talked about. She flew around the store, hanging up clothes and finding the right size, color, or style match for the customers. The hours of the day slipped by without Sharon noticing until suddenly she did not feel well. Dizziness, fatigue, headache, and nausea set in, and her legs went out from under her. Sharon had hit the glass ceiling and she had hit it hard. When you have gone that far, it takes days in bed to recover. Sharon went into a state of hyperarousal all day and then took a nose dive into hypoarousal. She did not step out of the activity when her body needed her to, so her body took her out of the activity when it was too much.

At the same time, I was working with a woman, older than Sharon, who had already learned the meaning of the word rest. Gerri really got the meaning of the glass ceiling and continually checked herself and adjusted her pace. She rested in her car before and after activities, sat quietly in the corner of the bookstore, or found the sofa in the department store. She knew all the spots in town where she could let her body step away from the glass ceiling so that she did not have to hit it to find out where it was. She had learned to read the Brain-Body Compass and had become an expert at fine-tuning its guidance.

These contrasting stories of how two women handled their autonomic nervous systems illustrate the benefit of managing your glass ceiling. As you sense your limitations and learn to regulate your activity, your cognition increases, your mood stabilizes, and your productivity expands. That is why I call optimal arousal an Expansion Zone. This is the fertile ground.

When the cingulate in the frontal lobe is strong enough to wait and working memory is strong enough to hold an awareness of the information in mind and then inhibit a reflexive reaction while paying attention to the emotion, life events can be a conscious choice with perspective on where you want to go. Living in the survival zone, constantly in hyperarousal, is very different than living in the Expansion Zone. The state of hyperarousal can protect you when there is danger, but if you stay too long in that state, your life can be diminished by the fallout effects. When you are in the optimal arousal state, you can use emotion to guide you to the expansion you seek and to be the fuel that sustains your efforts and expands your abilities when you have created the meaning for where you are going.

The trick to being awake to the regulation of your autonomic nervous system is to manage your glass ceiling. Don't get too tired, too hungry, too thirsty, or too angry. Exercise and release tensions as they build up. Focus on objects that will bring you joy and enhance your brain so that you can build the networks and balance the chemistry to produce the state you want. The glass ceiling is always moving, and the width of the Expansion Zone, where optimal arousal resonates, changes and narrows as the day goes by, while frustration mounts and fatigue increases. Hence, you may be able to stay focused and effective throughout the workday, but once the demands ease and the guard is down, the Expansion Zone may be small upon arriving home. Then a very different dynamic can take place.

This raises a curious question: Why does negativity come out on those we love? If the Expansion Zone has narrowed to a slit over the day, just pulling into the driveway to see that no one has taken in the garbage cans can be enough to unleash the physical

tension of the day on those unsuspecting family members awaiting your arrival. Remember, the degree to which we love someone
is the degree to which we can be hurt by them and express that
hurt inappropriately. Doing something like going for a walk, taking a ride, or working out at the gym before going home can open
the window of optimal arousal wide and welcome loved ones in to
engage your best self.

The world and everyone in it look different from each of these
zones. Something wanted but not achieved can look good from
a state of optimal arousal and evoke a sense of challenge and
curiosity. You can feel OK about not having achieved it because
the possibility is real and feels inviting. In a hyperaroused state
of negativity, the same topic can elicit a very different response of
anger, frustration, and insecurity; you feel bad about not having
achieved it, which results in a feeling of lack rather than the feeling
of possibility about the same issue. The view from optimal arousal
leads to your best outcome and your best self. I have learned many
of these insights from the disabled. They have limited wiggle room
and greater consequences for their choices. They have taught me
about dealing with adversity because they cannot walk away from
it, and when they find the way, the rest of us can follow.

Does Gender Make a Difference in the Stress Response?

All this revealing neuroscience, like most of science, has been found
through studies done on men. Only in the last decade have there
been studies identifying women's unique nervous system responses
to stress.[1] Surprise! Men and women are different, and now that
women have reached the level of education and position to do
the research, we are looking at ourselves. The titles fight-or-flight

and "tend and befriend" capture the difference between how men and women respond to hyperarousal.

It turns out that women don't freak out quite the same as men. When challenges threaten and the switch for an emergency state is flipped in the body, women appear to go in the opposite direction. While men more often move into fight-or-flight in the presence of a threat, women seem to experience a different chemi - cal activation, which moves them into their classical role of nurturing and produces behavior of tending to others' needs and befriending those challenged. In fact, it looks like the chemical oxytocin, the hormone released during childbirth, breastfeeding, and orgasm, is also released during times of stress, producing a strong desire to nurture and protect. A feeling of calm, focus, and caring causes women to experience less anxiety and orients them toward assisting and stabilizing others. This is because oxytocin reduces the hyperarousal of the sympathetic nervous system and HPAA activity.

The contrasting reactions for men and women under stress seem overall to be a brilliant balancing act in nature. In real emergencies, men are oriented toward the problem and women are oriented to caring for the people—a good basis for survival. One of the dynamics that I have seen with clients who are parents, is that the moment when both the fight-or-flight response and the "tend and befriend" response go awry simultaneously, the children are caught the middle, confused. When Dad is overreacting with fight-or-flight and getting scary and Mom starts overindulging with "tend and befriend" in an effort to stabilize, there is one bemused child. This is when the hyperarousal state changes perception and thinking, with each person convinced that he or she is right and the other is the cause of a spoiled, overindulged, or scared child.

Ladies, manage your oxytocin. Women often over-tend when they are out of balance. Then their own needs are no longer part of the equation. Check regularly on your own well-being and keep that in balance first. Enjoy your life. Stay confident in the potential of others to care for themselves. Dysregulated women forget to eat, or overeat and become overloaded emotionally and physically in their race to keep up with meeting everyone else's needs. Some of them have come to my office for neuropsychological evaluations for themselves because they've worn themselves out trying to keep track of the complexity of the lives of their children and husband. They are focused on the lives of their partner and children and have no measure of how much guidance is enough. The popular press calls them "helicopter parents" because they hover so much. In a lifestyle characterized by abundance, when there are limitless options, how do you know when to say no? How many activities are enough for the children? What are the signs you have left yourself and your well-being out of the list for the day?

If you have children, don't over-involve yourself in their lives. They have to figure it out. Making mistakes is part of living, learning, and becoming who you are. Discovering what does not feel good is part of learning to read the Brain-Body Compass, which they will use for guidance when they are not with you and must make decisions on their own. Believe in them, contribute to them, and stay in the Expansion Zone for you and everyone around you. Then you will be able to cheer them on without jumping in.

Women must also learn to say no as they transition into the workplace and still run households, raise children, and participate in the community. Making room to recognize the wisdom of the body when enough is enough is the frontier that currently remains blurred and can only be detected by a woman's own glass ceiling. Keeping up with male counterparts and doing it their way is not the answer.

Let others take on responsibility, even if they don't do it your way. Value the growth of others more than the perfection of the outcome. Learn to let go, make friends you enjoy, and be open to receiving from anyone and everyone. Have fun, read your own compass, and do what you need to keep expanding yourself.

Just as women can be overly focused on relationships, men can be very task oriented and less relational. This is a function of our different chemistry. The influence of women can help men be more aware of the implications of their actions for the process of the person involved, not just to complete the task.

While every brain is different and we do not all perfectly fit the characteristics of the male brain or female brain, being aware of the biological tendencies of your gender can help guide you as you become familiar with your glass ceiling and the fluctuations of your own autonomic nervous system.

Seeing through Pilgrim Eyes to Align Spirit, Brain, and Emotion

The quote on my calendar one day was "Life is 10 percent what happens to you and 90 percent how you respond to it," signed by that brilliant source, Anonymous. Now, that is a perspective from deep within the Expansion Zone on a really good day. Those who can get there and stay there long enough to align with their heart's desire can transcend any difficulty. The people I have known who can do this are utterly inspiring to me and have taught me a perspective I have called on in my darker moments.

One such time in my life was following my mother's transition from this earthly existence. At that point, much of my life's vision had been completed and mostly I felt as if I were out at sea, being blown by the wind. After six months of kindness to myself, I approached one of my best friends at Maryknoll, Sister Pat Murray, and asked her if she would like to go on a trip to Asia. I needed to get away. Sister Pat and I had traveled well together to Nicaragua, where she had lived for many years during the revolution, and to Africa to teach for the sisters who were assisting the Rwandan refugees who had come to Kenya. She has the great gift of a sense of humor and a broad perspective on the world. A mutual friend, Sister Dolores Geier, heard of our plans and gave us each a book as a traveling companion. *The Art of Pilgrimage* by Phil Cousineau was a great gift and the perfect tour guide.[2] A pilgrimage was just what I was seeking, but I did not know to call it that.

Looking back at that transformative time in my life, it is best described as "learning to see with pilgrim eyes." A pilgrimage is an inner journey, reaching beyond the surface of the physical place and time to arrive at a deeper inner resonance with what is really important. At a time of life transition, this is what I was seeking. Each day on a pilgrimage means choosing to step into the adventure of self-expansion best found in coming from a soul perspective, which offers change from the roots. Travel that gives you a sense of the spirit of the place connects you with your own spirit's expansion. A pilgrimage is essentially a search for the sacred and requires the eyes that are able to perceive and reveal meaning and purpose in life. This is why traveling to Asia, with its ancient spiritual traditions that I had never seen, could so totally open my eyes. A pilgrimage is travel undertaken from the soul reaching for wonder and open to discovery, a soul ready to move.

The art of pilgrimage is in perfecting the ability to step into each day with new eyes, detecting the Presence of the Sacred and honing a skill for discovery. Your luggage must contain a letting go of having the answers and an openness to receiving the questions that will guide you to a new place within yourself where your sacred aliveness awaits. The Presence of the Sacred renews and enlivens the spirit that longs for expansion. For me it was all about learning to step into the next phase of my life—newly, freshly, freely. Learning to access the eyes of a pilgrim means connecting the brain to the eyes of the heart and the soul and, from the perceptions of those eyes, finding meaning in a life worth living. That is the prize for which pilgrims travel—movement within to the rich inner land awaiting.

As a neuropsychologist, I have begun to think of pilgrim eyes as an "expect and detect" response in the nervous system, which reaches out, through the brain, from the soul. I have learned it is my choice to orient to the sensations and emotions of the Brain-Body Compass within me that can guide me to a connection with my heart and sacred meaning. The Expansion Zone, a state of optimal arousal, seems to me to have a depth to it where consciousness, emotion, and spirit can come together. I am never more easily able to shift out of unwanted emotions to an uplifted state than when I am viewing the world with pilgrim eyes.

This shift in emotion, despite no change in the external circumstances, is the power of focus and choice in self-regulation. My mother's transition at ninety-two years old was the normal course of events and to be expected. But on her passing, an energy in me passed on as well. She was a source of unconditional love for me, and in that relationship I found stability, appreciation, accomplishment, and possibility. She saw me as being able to do

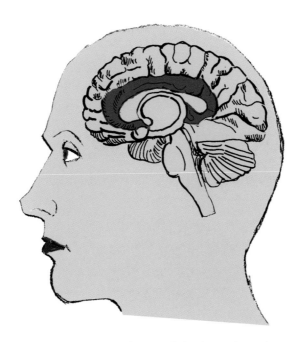

Figure 3.1 The cingulate: regulating focused attention

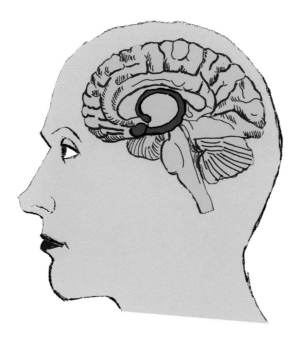

Figure 3.4 The limbic system: regulating your emotions

A

Autonomic Nervous System

PARASYMPATHETIC   **SYMPATHETIC**

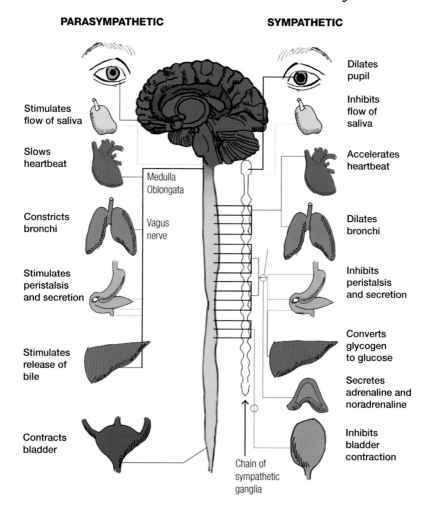

Stimulates flow of saliva

Slows heartbeat

Constricts bronchi

Stimulates peristalsis and secretion

Stimulates release of bile

Contracts bladder

Medulla Oblongata

Vagus nerve

Chain of sympathetic ganglia

Dilates pupil

Inhibits flow of saliva

Accelerates heartbeat

Dilates bronchi

Inhibits peristalsis and secretion

Converts glycogen to glucose

Secretes adrenaline and noradrenaline

Inhibits bladder contraction

Figure 3.5 Autonomic Nervous System: regulating sensation and emotion

B

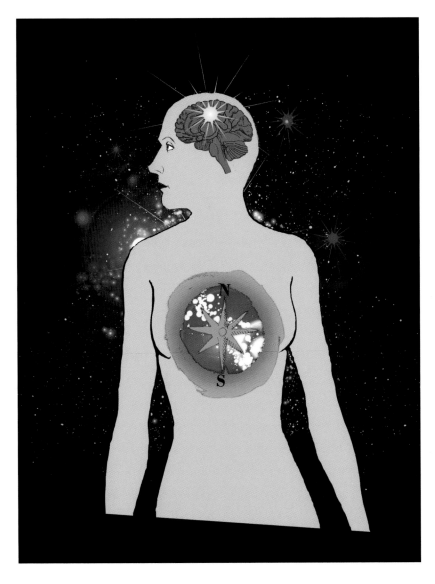

Figure 3.6 The Brain-Body Compass: the brain awake to sensation and emotion

The Maryknoll Sisters Motherhouse, built in 1932, is the center for training and sending sisters to the missions as well as their home upon returning from foreign lands. The architecture is in the Romanesque style, built in a square with an open courtyard in the center.

Winter picture of the Our Lady of Lourdes Grotto. In 1937, a replica of the Lourdes Grotto in France was built as a memorial. In former years, the expansive lawn in front of the grotto was used for the mission-sending ceremonies as the sisters left the United States for foreign lands.

D

Maryknoll novices and professed sisters chanting the Divine Office
in the Motherhouse Chapel in 1955.

Maryknoll Sisters Motherhouse Chapel on Sunday, August 7, 2011,
as the sisters rejoice during the recessional after mass.

Sister Susan Glass, MM, has been working as an educator in China for thirty years. Here she is teaching English to seventh-grade students at a school in Macau, China, in 2011.

Statue of Our Lady in the Garden of the Beatitudes on the grounds of the Maryknoll Sisters Center in New York.

The inner courtyard of the motherhouse contains vaulted arches, piers, quarry tiles on the walkway, and other decorative elements related to the Romanesque style to create a lovely, integrated garden space for prayerful reflection and outdoor enjoyment.

Sister Bernice Kita, MM, with the native women she teaches, who are cleaning coffee beans from the local harvest in Chajul, Guatemala, in 2010.

G

Sister Ann Hayden, MM, (top row, second left) visiting young women of the Maasai tribe who attend the Maryknoll EMUSOI Center, which promotes literacy for girls, run by Sister Mary Vertucci, MM, (top row, second right) in Arusha, Tanzania, in 2010.

anything I set my mind to. When we talked on the phone, I moved easily into this state she perceived in me. Somehow, being in her presence brought forth my possibility. We find dimensions of ourselves in the circumstances and relationships that call them forth. I wanted to find new doors that could again open the deeper recesses of my aliveness. When you have had the gift of unconditional love and you lose it, you know the well has run dry and it is time to look elsewhere. I was old enough to know I had to look within and needed to get out of the landscape that pulled my thoughts to the past.

As I prepared for my pilgrimage in southeast Asia, a book title captured my interest: *Losing Your Parents, Finding Yourself.*[3] The title said it all. It does not matter if your parents are fun or frustrating; when they go, it's up to you to make your own way. My friend Mimi says the ancient Hawaiian wisdom claims that after your parents leave, their best qualities can come out in you. That is what this whole book is about. You must dig deeply within yourself for your best qualities to surface. Their legacy awaits you there. This notion conveys the spirit of my pilgrimage to southeast Asia with Sister Pat. I chose to see with pilgrim eyes, to make an internal transition of my own and find my most essential self. Choosing to come from the place in yourself with pilgrim eyes when traveling in new lands with different cultures awakens your brain to see beyond the surface. Then you have a treasure within you to bring home.

Choosing the Conductor of the Orchestra

A young man who had been injured in a car crash on prom night came to my office after getting out of rehabilitation. He received therapy from me only for a short time, but his mother, Marcia, made a lasting impression on me. She had already lost one son and did not want to lose another. At Christmastime she dropped off a gift—a small box in the shape of a star—that contained holiday goodies. I commented on the box, and she told me that the star was an image that was very powerful for her. After her older son died, she found herself using them often to decorate—on her stationery, in her jewelry. She explained the star was a symbol of hope and possibility for her. When you make a wish on a star, it will come true. Just looking at a star was renewing for her and generated a sense of possibility in her body. It was her way of reading her Brain-Body Compass and regulating her autonomic nervous system to stay in the Expansion Zone despite some big challenges. The men in her life were risk takers, and she had to tolerate their risks, win or lose.

Marcia made a neurochoice about who would be the conductor of her orchestra, and she used stars as reminders to return to her Expansion Zone whenever life bounced her out. When we are paying attention, this is the choice we have. The brain has many functions, which together create different states. It is like an orchestra with different instruments—you are the one who determines which one will lead the way and what tune you will sing. Marcia was determined to be happy and used every trick she had to orient herself to staying there.

Marcia regularly goes to yoga class, is active in a knitting club, and is an avid museum-goer. When her son was going through a life-threatening event, she never wavered from her commitment to these practices. Usually these are called recreation and not given a high priority. If you think about the word *recreation*, you see re-create, because you find your own joy and stability there.

They kept her stable in an unstable time. They kept her emotions and nervous system in the Expansion Zone where she could think and be effective when it was important. Taking care of herself was her greatest expression of love for them. This is the only way you can offer your best self to those you love.

Over the centuries, many sources of meaning have been created in an attempt to explain suffering. Buddha told us that all life is suffering, and accepting that is the path to freedom from it. For some, suffering reflects punishment for bad deeds. For others, each struggle is a means for earning redemption and expanding in growth. In Christianity, the suffering of Jesus was an expression of love for humanity and a demonstration of the human capacity to transcend and transform suffering. The brain is always searching for meaning. It likes an explanation that brings coherence and alignment of the inner world. Reconciling conflicting thoughts and emotions with some overarching concept brings a focus and direction to thought and action. Each of us must decide for ourselves which meaning resonates as true within us.

Activate an Openness to the Rich Resources Within

Thinking from a perspective of making a neurochoice can open the doors to what is called spirituality. What is it? How does it work with the brain and body and how does it affect our emotions? Those are questions that have always fascinated me. As I have participated in the recovery process of people with traumatic brain injury, those who could access a spiritual meaning to turn to as a source of strength to stabilize their emotions and focus their attention are the ones who have always done the best. It doesn't seem to matter what religion or words they use; what matters is the effect of the meaning that stabilizes the emotions and creates a climate of hope within.

What is spirituality? My best descriptors of this elusive dimension have to do with an awareness of the inner source of strength opening a path to where the future can be viewed. It is the dimension where a person's deepest values and meanings reside and can be felt physically. This is the place to return to for reading your Brain-Body Compass and stabilizing your emotions. All the cultural and religious traditions describe this deep well of spiritual strength as a dimension of our being that we can expand with practices like meditation, prayer, and religious ritual. It is also stabilized and strengthened by the depth of meaning we choose to create and by the repetitive practice of focusing on that meaning.

Spiritual practices include those Marcia adheres to, enabling her to find the inner strength to assist those she loves. Looking at stars helps her KNOW she can do it; knitting gives her body and brain the respite and harmony of those rhythmic movements; going to museums allows her to be inspired by beauty; and doing yoga expands her physical well-being through stretching and the release of physical tension. These can all be ways of entering, expanding, and connecting with the deep well of resources available within.

These observations have spoken to me in many ways over the years, and the opportunities keep expanding. Now we have laughing yoga, very intricate breath work that regulates different parts of the nervous system, mindfulness meditation that slows the chatter of thoughts, dance to awaken the body's joyous energy store, and lots of forms of play that can be interpersonal or technological, with a wide range of apps available for your taste. All these will release you from hyperarousal or hypoarousal and activate an openness to the rich resources within. Each choice will create an inner chemistry you can produce, flavoring your emotions and perceptions of the world.

Some people turn to therapy to tap into this ability to shift an emotional state and be released from hyperarousal. However, many people come into my office with a very different view of the process. My client Ed had suffered a brain tumor, the removal of which left his cognitive skills decreased. He came for treatment after a couple of years on disability. He wanted to go back to work and was young enough to do so if his skills could be improved, but he was angry and resentful that this had happened to him. He had come from humble beginnings and had achieved the good life, and now he had lost the dream he had created. I told Ed it was time to stop talking about his reactions and focus on the solutions we could offer. Ed looked at me in a very puzzled way and said, "I thought therapy was a chance to vent about the problems and then they gave you drugs." No one had put it quite so bluntly as Ed, but this is a lot of what I have seen go on in the mental health field.

I have learned to meditate with people for a few minutes at the beginning of the session because they come in deeply entrenched in the hyperarousal state, in which no productive thinking is possible. By sitting in silence—breathing, scanning the body for tensions, and releasing them so that ease can return—the brain and the thoughts it produces can be released from the grip of negativity, and solutions can then be unearthed. Solutions are always waiting beneath the surface if stillness is available and listening is possible. Talking about the problem builds the neural network around the problem, while talking only about solutions builds new neural networks that strengthen skills. This applies whether you are in a therapy situation or you are simply discussing what's going on in your life with friends and family. How you choose to think about things changes the outcome.

The real value of a therapeutic relationship—whether with a literal therapist or a loved one who supports you—is that it helps you see what is possible. For example, sometimes my patients need education about the brain or strategies for dealing with cognitive limitations and ways of stepping back from stress. Sometimes my ability to maintain my own emotional stability while talking about issues that create emotional upheaval in them is the beginning of their ability to get perspective. Sometimes I tell them my story about my sister's brain injury from the perspective of having gotten through it rather than being in the middle of it. While it is by no means the only way to achieve perspective, therapy offers a context in which a person can find hope and direction. The relationship is a stable context or platform for developing a new story to tell. When the relationship works, it's because something happens between the patient and therapist that enables a person to see what's possible.

My goal—as a therapist and author—is to help people learn to entrain their nervous system to a stable level of arousal in the face of any challenging topic so that they will be more effective in achieving their goals. Getting a glimpse of the action going on within your brain changes everything in terms of exploring, recognizing, and managing the world of emotion. From there you get yourself into a state where you can recognize and manage your own emotions and use the information they are giving you to create your life.

When people are awake to how this works, body sensation becomes information on the compass, showing them what to move away from and what to move toward. A greater sense of confidence arises and a vision of what is possible becomes more real. This is the platform of power available in working memory when we get past negative emotion and use the cingulate to focus and make it real. Sports psychology is especially powerful in making this platform available. Athletes take time to imagine what they want. Skiers see themselves skiing down the mountain before they go. They prime their brain for the best outcome and pave the way for the neurons to produce what their imagination can see.

It's all about keeping the executive operating officer up to the job. When the cingulate can stay focused on the possibility because the nervous system is humming, all the instruments in your orchestra will play the tune you want to hear. Meditation exercises and strengthens the cingulate, and learning to recognize the sensations of emotion can be the perfect guide to where you want to go.

During the Great Depression, a very traumatic time in our history, Franklin Delano Roosevelt campaigned for the job of president of the United States. Upon being elected, he emphatically declared that the "only thing we have to fear is fear itself." Looking back at the impact those words had on the United States and knowing what we do now about the effect of fear on our ability to access our best selves, we know even more precisely the power and wisdom of his leadership vision and the benefits of that thinking for everyone.

Awakening Applications

• Learn to see with the eyes of expectancy. Then learn to develop your "expect and detect" response. Once you set an intention in your brain, your body recognizes the sensation of the emotions that bring you closer to your goal and guide you forward. If journaling helps you set your intentions, commit them to paper in your journal. Record your intentions, what you expect your outcome to be, and how your body feels when you imagine it happening. Your Brain-Body Compass will lead you there.

- The optimal arousal state—or the Expansion Zone—is where you access your best self. How do you get and stay in your optimal arousal state? Exercise and release tensions as they build up. Keep up adequate nutrition, hydration, and sleep. Focus on objects that remind you of pleasant, hopeful memories and enhance your brain to build the networks and balance the chemistry to produce the state you want. Take frequent breaks when you find yourself in stressful situations.

- You have within you a deep well of spiritual strength where you can return to regulate your autonomic nervous system and stabilize your emotions. Practices like meditation, prayer, and religious ritual offer the kind of repetition that strengthens your access to your spiritual self. I provided some basic forms of meditation in chapter 2; here I offer one that addresses your body tensions when emotions need regulating: First, close your eyes and sit comfortably, relaxing into the chair. Let your breath go deeply into your diaphragm while also filling your upper lungs. As you regulate your breath, begin to scan your body from top to bottom, noticing any sense of tension or tightness. Then imagine that you are breathing into your head on the in breath, and on the out breath allow the tension to melt away, flowing down and out of your body. Gradually move down to your face and neck, scanning for tight muscles and allowing them to release. It takes very little time to repeat this practice as you move down your shoulders, back, chest, belly, hips, legs, and feet. Some people like remembering the feeling of standing in the shower and having the water pouring over them as they imagine the tension flowing down and out of their body. When you take the time to let go of the tension in your body, collected over the course of the day, you enhance your own experience going forward.

Notes

1. Shelley Taylor, *The Tending Instinct* (New York: Henry Holt, 2002).

2. Phil Cousineau, *The Art of Pilgrimage* (Berkeley: Conari Press, 2000).

3. Victoria Secunda, *Losing Your Parents, Finding Yourself* (New York: Hyperion, 2000).

6

A Neuropsychological
Treatment Model

When I give presentations on neuropsychology, the majority
of the audience has questions about how our brains function.
Whether or not the people I speak to have difficulty with their
brain function, they almost always know someone who is affected:
people struggling with age-related memory problems, a brain
injury, "chemo brain," sports-related concussions, post-traumatic
stress disorder, learning disabilities, or failure to reach academic
benchmarks like passing the bar exam, just to name a few.

Millions of people are affected by these challenges, and if you
are one of them I'd like to use this chapter to describe the unique
treatment model I have developed over the years, which has
helped people successfully confront their brain limitations. If you
are not struggling with your brain function, you might want to
skip this chapter, although I would still encourage you to read it
if you know someone who could benefit from your understanding of treatment possibilities or if you yourself are interested in

learning more about the ways our brains can grow and change. Even well-functioning, healthy brains have the ability to expand and awaken to greater potential and benefit from the same principles discussed here.

My Approach to Neuropsychological Therapy

When I first started treating brain injuries, I had had extensive experience in diagnosis and treatment in both graduate school and postdoctoral training. It did not take long for me to see that the complexity of brain injury was beyond my scope as a sole practitioner. That was when I started looking for other professionals who were trained in an understanding of brain function and rehabilitation and had the heart to create a better way to help. It takes a whole village to recognize and participate in this phoenix rising from the ashes. When the whole village comes together, magic happens, and that's what we do at my practice, Neuropsychological Services of Westchester, New York (NSW).

The process of giving a crash course in neuropsychology as part of the treatment, which I discussed in chapter 2, has evolved over time. Back in the 1980s when I started, we knew much less than we do now, and I was initially trained to take a testing approach, for diagnostic and treatment purposes, rather than an educational approach. But over time, I saw how much change occurred just by explaining to my patients things like working memory and cognitive style. Essentially, we are still asking the same questions when patients come to the office with concerns about their brains. Something in cognitive processing is not working well, but now we can do a lot more than just give a diagnosis. We can help patients learn a language to describe, explain, and solve the problem. Science is expanding daily in its ability to explain what it all means and how to work with it.

Although a focus on where you are going is the most productive approach to achieving change, a good starting point is a thorough understanding of where you are. The initial evaluation for sorting out neuropsychological function takes two to three days and includes tasks that engage the language system, visual system, motor system, memory, attention, executive functions, academic skills, and personality development. Task performance is compared to that of others who are the same age so that a profile of peaks and valleys emerges. Everyone is better at some things than others.

After the tests are administered and scored, it is time to talk about the findings. The most relevant way of pulling out the value from the data is to focus on the problem under this new lamppost, shining a light and looking for the solutions. This is where the crash course in neuropsychology begins. By discussing how a particular pattern of cognitive strengths and weaknesses produced the problem, we can begin to see the solution.

In treating an injury to the brain, there are eight dimensions to grasping the problem, designing the treatment, and making the necessary guidance available to reach a new and happier place in life. The most complex treatment we offer is the neuropsychological model for brain rehabilitation after trauma.

To illustrate the eight dimensions of brain injury treatment, I'll use the example of one of my patients, Ray, and his journey through treatment. Not many of my patients share all of Ray's challenges; his situation was extreme and he did well despite it. Other patients have one or more of his challenges. But his story represents what is possible in the extreme, which is hopeful for the rest of us.

THE EIGHT DIMENSIONS OF BRAIN INJURY TREATMENT AT NSW

Neuropsychological evaluation	Family therapy
Individual psychotherapy	Behavior modification
Stress management	Group therapy
Cognitive rehabilitation	Community integration

Ray was a lawyer and had enjoyed a highly successful career until he hit a deer while driving on the highway and suffered a significant brain injury, primarily to his right hemisphere. As mentioned before, right hemisphere injuries prevent people from integrating new information into old concepts. If a right hemisphere injury is located in just the right spot, the result is anosognosia, the inability to be aware of changes in oneself. When that happens, people continue to function on old news, unable to adapt to the new news. This includes key dimensions of who they are and how they live. Although no longer working or bringing in an income, they continue to live in the past (for example, spending money from the budget they had established with a high salary). Unmet commitments and relationship disappointments are often due to the entrenched self-concept established pre-injury, which has not changed to accommodate the post-injury circumstances.

Ray struggled with this syndrome. Immediately after his injury, he had the attitude that he was in charge and, upon discharge from the hospital, did not see the point in further therapy. Ray was totally focused on getting back to work, which he did.

I did not see Ray until fifteen years after his brain injury. Despite the life-threatening injury, his left hemisphere remained strong. The problem was the right. He had lost perspective of the big picture and the ability to adapt to change—something he had always been good at. Because his left hemisphere was so strong, it was hard to argue with him. He had an answer for everything. Unfortunately, he did not listen or accept help until he ran out of answers.

When Ray came to my office with his brother, he had been through a lot. He had lost his job, his wife had divorced him, he had alienated his children, and he had lost a few more jobs after that. When his house was repossessed, Ray moved in with his mother. When she died, he had no more answers. He was learning the hard way. Finally he was willing to come for treatment and try to adjust to creating a new life for who he was now. Here is the story of Ray's treatment process, starting from his initial evaluation and ending with his successful reintegration back into his community.

Neuropsychological Evaluation

Starting with the neuropsychological evaluation provides an understanding of the cognitive strengths and weaknesses. It also enables the rest of the treatment to capitalize on the person's strengths to expand the skills for mastery in the identified challenges. The neuropsychological testing provides a map for understanding the many levels of human function (e.g., cognitive strengths and challenges, emotional awareness and regulation, behavioral or lifestyle influences that are limiting or enhancing, family support or challenge, social skills and community support, psychological stability and limitations, functional and dysfunctional types of interaction). Once the problem is precisely defined, the path to the solution becomes apparent.

The crash course in neuropsychology continues throughout treatment, and we approach all treatment at NSW in an educational way. The ability for treatment to generalize to expand daily life skills and successful activities depends on the degree of understanding a person has about **why** they are doing things and awareness of **how** they are learning to do them differently. In this sense, psychotherapy is oriented toward learning about how the brain works, the different cognitive skills and their effectiveness, the ability of emotion to enhance, sustain, or limit focus and skill level, relationship dynamics, and ways of managing behavior.

After seeing his performance on the neuropsychological tests, Ray started to comprehend that his problems could not be blamed on everyone else; they had something to do with him. Slowly, awareness was expanding and a new light was dawning. This was the beginning. Without that level of consciousness, there is no change in behavior. Ray was ready to move from initial evaluation to psychotherapy.

Individual Psychotherapy

The most important part of individual psychotherapy is learning to tell a new story about the experience, one that focuses on where the person is going rather than where he or she has been. This includes creating new meaning for the circumstance and benefiting from the sense of purpose that comes from it. In Ray's case, explanations were essential to engage him in change. When Ray did the tasks on the neuropsychological testing, he saw the things he could not do. That was when Ray finally started to understand his part in the problems he'd had over the years—and what he could do about it. In therapy, a patient's primary goal is to integrate the gains achieved in the different treatments in a way that allows the person to understand and access them when needed. Being able to use the new skills outside of treatment means that the skill is really theirs. Hence, some amount of psychotherapy is integrated into all the other modalities to enhance awareness and provide integration of these new skills.

Stress Management Treatment

Stress management treatment of the autonomic nervous system addresses all the issues about dysregulated emotion discussed in chapters 4 and 5. Ray had developed a short fuse and a strong reactivity over the years. When he got uncomfortable, he quickly went into fight-or-flight, and he did not have any control over that response. His explosive temper cost him his family and his career. Slowly his emotional outbursts burnt the bridges of relationships in his life until there was only his mother and brother. Then there was only his brother, who had learned to set boundaries in the relationship. This meant our first goal for Ray was stress management treatment with Dr. Jay, my business partner, who is responsible for the neuropsychological evaluations and stress management treatment at NSW. He uses biofeedback equipment to measure skin response, heart rate, and skin temperature, which indicate a person's levels of physiological arousal at the time they are feeling and discussing the events in their life.

This combination creates an awareness of the level of emotion and its meaning in the moment. It is an opportunity to observe how the thoughts and emotions are surfacing in the body. These reactions were so practiced that Ray did not even realize he was yelling. In fact, he was shocked when he began to recognize how often his fight-or-flight response was activated. Ray discussed how emotional explosions happened in lots of places. His only coping strategy was to yell or to remove himself from the situation. There were stores in town where he could not go because he had burnt the bridges there with his fight response. In the grocery store, he consistently had trouble using the credit card swipe and would get so frustrated with turning the card around and around that he would leave all the groceries on the conveyor belt and bolt out of the store. He did not want to yell, since he knew he would need groceries again and would have to go back.

As Ray and Dr. Jay discussed episodes such as these, Dr. Jay would point out the spikes on the computer that indicated Ray's hyperarousal state. Dr. Jay would then ask about the emotional feelings and physical sensations Ray was having, and Ray could then recognize and learn to regulate them. Dr. Jay teaches three ways to reduce the physical signs of stress. Isometric exercises enabled Ray to release tension in his neck and back as it built up. Positive self-statements, like words that anticipate success rather than fear of failure, orient the brain to the best possible outcome. Learning to breathe at a rate that slows the heart restores a sense of calm and enhances a broader, more effective perspective. With continued therapy, Ray began to recognize the bodily sensations that told him trouble was brewing, and released them. Eventually he was able to ask for help with the swipe and even laugh at these stumbling blocks as he got used to them under calmer conditions.

When you regulate feelings before you act, they are still in your conscious control. When Ray was finally able to recognize the sensations in his body, he could then begin to learn to regulate his reactions. When you recognize and regulate your emotions, they do not determine your experience or what you say or do;

instead, they are information. Then you are awake to what your nervous system is telling you and you are able to make a neuro-choice about what you want.

Cognitive Rehabilitation

Training cognitive skills can be stressful, even if you understand the goal and recognize your reactions. Ray worked for a long time to grasp how the injury affected him and learn the methods for soothing himself when the fight-or-flight response went off. He learned to tolerate and acknowledge the limits of his ability in order to go beyond the dysfunction in his life. In cognitive rehabilitation sessions with his therapist, Ray needed training in all attention types—focused, sustained, alternating, and divided. He did exercises to expand his working memory so that he could hold on to his train of thought and keep an eye on his goal. His right hemisphere injury limited his visual, spatial, and constructional skills as well as his awareness of the big picture in life. Once he could grasp the value of the cognitive rehabilitation and control his reactions, Ray did well in the tasks that strengthened his cognitive ability. He came each week for a workout in the "brain gym" with his cognitive rehabilitation therapist, who had a great sense of humor and kept Ray laughing.

Learning new approaches and doing repetitive exercises to master a skill can feel like either a challenge to be accomplished or a source of constant judgment and criticism. This is where regulating the emotion is essential and telling a new story is imperative. The neurochoice you make about where you are coming from definitely determines whether you come back for another session and whether you see the therapist or doctor as teacher or torturer. We do the same exercises in each person's session, but patients often tell themselves very different stories. When a person approaches a task with the desire to surpass the last score and can tolerate mistakes, the brain adapts and grows. Treating awareness is an essential component to success in cognitive rehabilitation and is part of every conversation in treatment.

Family Therapy

Family members face their own trauma and adjustment when a brain injury happens to a loved one. It often means twice the work for the family member, as well as a huge loss of income and support. They don't always know which of their loved one's difficult behaviors are a result of the injury and they don't know how to be constructive in handling them. Families need their own assistance in this adjustment, and if they are not doing well, no one else will either. They are the ones who keep the household going, pay the bills, and keep track of everything that the person with the injury can't. Treatment does not work well if family members are not doing well. They come for their own session and are given the crash course in neuropsychology, along with coaching in how to pace themselves, when to intervene, and when to let go.

Behavior Modification

Along with emotional and cognitive challenges, lots of behavioral problems result from a brain injury. Problems with keeping appointments on time, sticking to a regular eating and sleeping schedule, and being organized with materials and routines all surface when the brain is injured. These behaviors are based in the executive functions of the brain (see the Executive Functions box in chapter 3). Each of these is readily addressed by designing behavioral plans, using calendars to structure time and activities, and providing repetitive reinforcement to assist the patient in establishing new patterns of behavior better suited to supporting brain function, health, and achievement. The plan itself is established in the psychotherapy treatment and then reinforced in all the modalities. We gradually discuss the plan in psychotherapy. We then explore, design, and reinforce strategies in cognitive rehabilitation, while stress management treatment helps mitigate the frustrations of carrying out the strategies. Many times family members use reminders and encouragement at home to facilitate the training of new behaviors. This gives them a constructive way to approach their frustrations and be part of the solution instead of, over time, becoming part of the problem.

In Ray's case, the lack of this type of integrated treatment model at the time of his injury resulted in divorce from his wife and alienation from his children. His mother and brother stuck by him over the years, and his brother participated in learning about the treatment. He talked to Ray about how to achieve his goals and encouraged him along the way. Ray did eventually reconnect with his adult children, who lived in other states. They likewise talked with me to better understand what to expect from him. Eventually Ray was able to share with his children a new understanding of the experiences that had been confusing all of them over the years, and he slowly formed new relationships with his family.

Group Therapy

Once a patient recovers from the brain injury to the point of having some objectivity about what happened and what the evaluation means, and having achieved some awareness and social skills in treatment, group therapy is appropriate. This allows people to receive the support of others who have also traveled this path and gain independent functioning in a new social setting. For two hours each week, Ray sat in a group with other adults who were also recovering from traumatic brain injuries. Ray listened to the events of their lives, learned to share his experience, and even laughed at himself as they did. In group therapy, the brain must put together all the skills of cognition, emotion, and interpersonal relating. This is where people get to see themselves overreact, underreact, miss the point, or be several steps behind the point, as well as reflect on the meaning of others' challenges and successes to learn what is possible for them.

Ray did well in group therapy, where he met others who faced similar challenges. Together they created a perspective and humor about many hurdles they faced. When the sensations of erupting rage went off in group therapy, Ray learned to get up, walk out of the room, go downstairs, and step outside to breathe fresh air. He knew he could not yell at anyone there, and he did not want to.

Community Reintegration

At this point in recovery, it was essential for Ray to grasp and use his executive functions. He had to form goals and intentions and sustain his focus on them despite other distractions. Ray started making decisions in anticipation of a future he wanted, not just in reaction to the moment. He could now hold all that in mind sufficiently to guide him. At this phase of the treatment, when people go into group therapy, they also undertake work trials. This usually means participating in volunteer work of their choosing. I encourage them to select some community involvement they are attracted to because they like the environment, people, cause, or tasks. The message is: do something you enjoy. This is a very interesting time in people's lives because most have not participated independently in the community since their injury and are often unsure of what they will like. They are also unsure of their skill set and of just how accurate it will turn out to be. Ray was not going back to work, so he chose to volunteer in a beautiful, serene Asian garden. He found the weeding and planting soothing to his nerves, and he enjoyed the contact with others who also loved the beauty of nature.

Over the years, I have seen lots of people go back too soon to their previous paid employment—and then get fired. Unfortunately, they can also lose their disability insurance as well, since they were cleared by their doctors as no longer disabled in order to return to work. These brutal experiences can be avoided when some exploration is done in a volunteering capacity to reveal a person's level of skill and reliability. Problems that arise in a volunteer setting become information to guide the treatment so that the patient can meet challenges successfully.

When these eight dimensions of therapy come together, we find success. I specifically remember the day that Ray realized he was connecting the neuronal dots. In group therapy, he told us of driving along a side street in his neighborhood when someone pulled out in front of him from a street on the right. Since his reaction time was slow, this kind of action always startled him and left him feeling like he was going to crash again. Ray laid his hand on the horn and started to yell and curse—a practiced response for a number of years. It was summertime and all of Ray's windows were open, so the sound of his voice carried. He had a big voice. As the other car drove away, it cleared his view, and he saw an older woman walking her dog just to the right of his car. Ray saw the startled look on her face and the fear in her body as she jumped back. She looked like his mother. Ray realized for the first time that he was hurting people he did not want to hurt. **Neurons that had not been connected for a long time finally spoke to each other.** That awareness changed how Ray saw the world and how he functioned in it.

Awareness is always the key to each and every meaningful change. Being aware of the information of his emotions helped Ray go back to the grocery store whenever he wanted, get to know new people in group therapy, slow down when driving, and be a part of his community. The sensations, thought, pacing, and coordination were all adapting because his awareness was guiding his focus.

Ray practiced breathing methods, imagined going into the grocery store and getting the swipe going in the right direction, made an effort to slow down and let others go ahead of him, and practiced receiving their appreciation. Ray finally connected the neuronal dots about what was important to him and started getting comfortable in the new skin he was living in. He started feeling comfortable walking in his neighborhood and one day ran into someone he had gone to high school with. They were both retired and she was now alone too. When I last saw Ray, he was going to the high-school reunion with her. He enjoyed making friends and venturing out of his solitary life instead of being afraid of the reactions he might have.

I offer you the story of Ray and of the treatments that enabled him to overcome his limitations fifteen years after his injury because I want you to grasp what is possible if you know how to engage neuroplasticity. According to what I learned in graduate school, everything Ray achieved was not possible at that late date. But people like Ray have shown us the power of neuroplasticity and belief. Ray finally decided to change his life and when he did, the limitations he had been living with changed. If it is possible for Ray, imagine what is possible for those of us who do not have his limitations. We just have to believe that we, too, can tap into that power.

Awakening Applications

- While this book is designed to give you the tools to start awakening your brain on your own through the use of neurochoice, you may be interested in a professional neuropsychological evaluation. Check my website, awakeningthebrain.com, for information on how to find a neuropsychologist in your area. For individual consultations, you can make an appointment with me on my website.

- If you are interested in applying the principles in this treatment model for yourself, think about the many dimensions of you that can be regulated. First determine what you want. Then practice stabilizing yourself in optimal arousal. Engage in tasks that will strengthen your mental skills, like attention or working-memory exercises. Develop a support group of people that can help keep you on track (be sure they have a sense of humor). Don't take score on your progress too often; just keep going on the path to your goal. The brain is like a muscle. If you give it a workout, it will get stronger.

7

Creating an Awakening Brain: The Role of Thought and Focus

After my mother's transition, an energy of urgency left me, and I realized how tired I felt. As I described in chapter 1, I knew that the body re-creates every cell over a seven-year period, so I decided to give myself seven years to learn to re-create my own physical health. It was time to practice what I preached to others. I knew all about the Brain-Body Compass but had not used it for my own health. In other words, I had been using it for others but not for myself. It was time to be deliberate about asking the questions that focused on creating wellness for myself and using the response I felt for guidance in achieving my goal.

I had been interested in the healing energy methods from Asia and started acupuncture to regain my energy. One day after my doctor had put in the needles, I lay on the table in the darkness, listening to the soft music and letting go of tension. I had a cold that had settled in my chest and a slight cough that I did not want to activate while I was full of needles. It is best not to move, if you know what I mean. Mostly, I focused on my breath moving in and out and enjoyed the relaxing music. As various thoughts came into my mind, I noticed sensations in my body and how they varied depending on the thought's meaning. Each time I thought about my appreciation for my doctor and the healing environment he had created, my muscles released and relaxed. Each time I thought of a patient, considering where to go next in his or her treatment, my muscles tightened up again. That was interesting. My body was following my thoughts.

Then the real surprise came. Each time I thought of a particular patient, Jack, who had suffered a brain injury but also had a history of significant trauma prior to the injury, I noticed that I physically felt a sense of worry. I had not worked with anyone like him before and I wanted to help him, but I felt unsure of how to address his complex history and current situation. As thoughts of Jack popped into my mind, I gently reminded myself that this was my time of rest and rejuvenation. Letting go of my thoughts, along with the inner climate they created, was part of obtaining the benefit of the session. So I let go of the thoughts and again enjoyed the music.

Interestingly, my concern for Jack kept coming back, and finally I noticed that every time I thought of him, my lungs tightened and I felt like I was going to cough. This was not a good idea when I was lying there full of needles. This completely grabbed my attention, and I became curious about how my thoughts affected my body. For the first time, I saw the physical manifestation of each of my thoughts, and it varied with the emotions I had about the topic. When my focus followed the music, muscles were released that I hadn't realized were tight. When I thought of Jack, I started to cough. The needles in my body were a powerful motivation to pay attention and control my focus, keeping it off the thoughts that contained resistance and shifting instead toward the ease and openness I was seeking.

There I was, lying in the dark, watching the impact of my thoughts on my body. That was the day I decided to always meditate in some mind-clearing way when doing this type of restorative work. Before, I had often let my mind wander wherever it went. But that day I realized that the health professionals I go to can only do half the job—and I must do the inside job. Getting a benefit from an acupuncture session or a massage or reflexology or any type of healing modality is only partly due to the professional. Part of the benefit depends on me, and I suspect that my part is the most important part. Jack did me a great favor that day. Being aware of when you are encountering what you don't want is half of the solution to finding what you do want, even in your thoughts.

How Neurochoice Builds the Neural Network of Meaning You Seek

There is a concept in neuropsychology called Theory of Mind, which is considered to be one of the brain's functions.[1] We all have a theory about what is in the minds of other people. After years of knowing each other, we think we know what is in the mind of our parents, children, partners, or colleagues. We develop a theory based on past experience of what they like and don't like and what they have or have not experienced in life. We have a theory about what is in their mind and in our own.

In your brain, that theory represents a neural network of connections that access many varied experiences you have had with and without another person, which is the basis for your interpretation of them. This Theory of Mind is part of what I am thinking about when I talk about the "eyes" you see with. Often we think we know what is going on with someone we have known well, only to discover a whole new dimension of their experience or thinking that is only now surfacing. Where we get in trouble is when we think we know what is happening and are no longer open to the growth and change in others, holding them back from moving into a new dimension of themselves because our theory of mind is not open to change.

The "eyes" of a scientist or an explorer, on the other hand, are looking for the signs of new discovery. This is the "how" of your focus in contrast to the "what" you focus on. Letting my mind wander during acupuncture had been a habit that often produced good insight into the meaning of conversations and ideas for treatment plans. But on that day, indulging in mind wandering was a whole new experience. I was developing a fresh theory about how my thoughts and emotions affect my body as I watched my muscles respond to those thoughts and emotions. It is often the experience we don't want that really gets our attention.

Because of that experience, the way I viewed my thoughts and my cough expanded my theory of my own mind, the role of emotions embedded in the thoughts, and the ability I had to influence my body. That insight gave me a whole new dimension of information for my theory about me and my ability to regulate myself. If you can be aware of your thoughts and the emotions they activate in your body, you can use that information to regulate your autonomic nervous system and stay in a state of optimal arousal.

Have there been times when you have felt sensations in your body as you anticipated something coming up in your day? If the sensations were exciting, inspiring, or hopeful, did it help to stay in touch with them as your day progressed until you got there? Having something to look forward to enhances everything else you are doing. If the thought turned your stomach, tightened your shoulders, or caused your heart to pound with anxiety, did you listen and let go of those sensations before engaging in the next thing? It doesn't work to your advantage to take an anticipated problem into an unrelated situation. Shift your state and focus on why you want to be where you are and give your best to it. Don't let your thoughts and emotions work against you. You can take charge of them.

This also leads me to thoughts on what it means to use only 10 percent of one's brain. When I am in a rejuvenating activity like acupuncture, which opens the flow of energy in my body, but I am entertaining worrisome thoughts that trigger body-tensing emotions, very little of my focus is on the reason I am there, and the internal climate I am creating is the opposite of my declared intention. My full brain is not accessing my full nervous system and body to align with my intention. Then I am actually working against myself by splitting my focus and applying only a small portion of my brain power, awareness, and felt sense to what I say I want. There is often a whole lot going on in there that we are completely unaware of but can awake to and direct.

Knowledge is power. **When you are sensitive enough to be aware of the emotional effects your thoughts have on your body, you are finally in a position to have some neurochoice about regulating that process in the direction of the outcome you want.** Now that you more fully understand what is going on in your brain and body, you have the ability to exercise neurochoice to do something about it.

Achieving an Intention by Focusing
on the Brain-Body Compass

As I discovered the relationship between cognition and emotion first-hand while lying on the acupuncture table, I could see my own habit of thought that shapes my emotional state and colors my perception of the world. This experience led me to reconsider how I was using my brain. I already had a long history of forming intentions and focusing on them. I had followed my dreams to become first a nun and then a doctor and developed a neuropsychology practice with an integrated treatment model. Now I wanted to engage that part of my brain that had been inaccessible to me because of wandering thoughts and random emotions. Staying solidly in the Optimal Arousal Zone leads to expansion if you form an intention and stay focused on it. I started to be aware of these dynamics on a whole new level after that experience. I learned that if my cognitive abilities could be applied to my intention and my focus could stay on the desired outcome, the Brain-Body Compass would guide me to where I wanted to go.

This is the essence of locating your North Star, the vision that guides you to your destination. The meaning of the intention is crucial to your ability to stay focused on your purpose. Despite how important recovery from brain injury has become in my life because of my career and my family, nothing has kept my attention quite like having to cough during acupuncture. That showed me what was possible in a way I cannot forget. I often think there is a place we come from after such experiences, like orienting to the "expect and detect" response I introduced in chapter 5 instead of the fight-or-flight response that can come up so easily. This is the "how" dimension of my focus. How I look at my experience depends on my intention for looking and what I have learned about the method of looking.

Siddhartha reinvented himself. He went from being a prince to being a Buddha. He focused on his North Star to find the path to overcoming suffering through meditation. His life had a singular purpose: to reach enlightenment and then teach others how to get there. Jesus came from the place of love within himself. That is his primary, consistent message. Love outweighs all else. Forgiveness returns you to your best self where love resides. He lived from that North Star, no matter what. The British psychologist John Bowlby tells us that we are happiest and most effective when we are aligned with those whom we trust and who are there to assist us.[2] He was sent away to boarding school at seven years old and went on to make a career of exploring the loss of connection that experience caused him and what could restore him to his best self.

Each of these people stayed focused on their North Star and went beyond what humanity knew in their time. Similarly, these are some of the things people learn about when they come for a neuropsychological evaluation: the relationship between their intention, thought habits, cognitive skills, and regulation of emotion. Together, these create your life. When emotion is dysregulated or habits of thought are unconscious and undirected, the intention gets lost.

The old recommendation to count to ten before you speak when you are upset really does give you the chance to get smarter and be more effective. This is what happens when primary process (raw, spontaneous emotion) is managed by secondary process (awareness, focus, cognition, and intention). Interrupting your own thoughts midstream when you realize that the old automatic chatter has taken over all the space in your head is an important skill to master. Meditation, where you gently release intrusive thoughts as you focus on your breath, strengthens the cingulate to be more and more effective in shifting your focus where you want it. A quiet mind can consider, reflect, and reason more effectively than a mind where 50 percent of the attention is occupied with chatter.

Lots of people who come for testing exhibit what we call negative self-talk: they are talking to themselves in a critical voice. Their mind is saying to them, "I can't do this," or "Oh no, I am really bad at that," or many other undermining statements that create a powerless emotion within. This is the opposite of the confident thinking that wonders how this works or what is the best way to do it. Is there a "blame and shame" response that takes over the brain with a chemistry that prevents us from applying ourselves? Is there a "reflect and adapt" response that provides the chemistry the brain needs for the confidence to persist in finding the answer?

Negative self-talk goes on all the time in people who do not even know their brain is doing it, and often it shuts them out of using skills they have. A better approach, which helps people access more of their brain, is to slow down, count to ten, observe and interrupt the negative self-talk, and keep expecting to find the answer. If you learn the feeling of being in charge of your thoughts and emotions and are willing to stay there, you will be guided to your North Star. This approach accesses more of your brain power.

Mollie Rogers, the founder of Maryknoll, is one of the people who knew how to do this. Back in 1912 she and six other women came together to provide secretarial services to a new effort in the

Catholic Church to promote assistance to less fortunate people in foreign countries. This was done with the support of the Catholic Church and was the first time men and women from the United States went out to contribute to developing countries. Mollie had a vision of contributing in foreign lands when she saw other young women at Smith College, who were from Protestant churches, participating in this effort. This was a vision that never left her and one she shared with many. Those seven women, along with the priests, Father Walsh and Father Price, shared a vision whose time had come.

Over the years since those seven women came together to make a dream a reality, 3,498 more women have come, myself included. But it takes someone to say it and do it and believe it can happen for others to join in and make a dream become reality. When I think about how one woman's vision called that many more to create a community, which for more than one hundred years has reached around the world to educate, feed, heal, soothe, and inspire peoples of forty nations, simply because she believed it was possible, I am inspired to trust my own vision and reach beyond what is here now.

Getting the Right and Left Hemispheres to Work Together

Often, getting free of mind chatter is called "quieting the left hemisphere," which is where language is localized for most people. The neuroanatomist Jill Bolte Taylor tells the story of her left hemisphere stroke. She talks movingly of changes in her experience as the bleed in the left side of her brain expanded, shutting down her language functions. All thought in language was going offline.

Jill Bolte Taylor describing the change in her consciousness from her left hemisphere stroke.
http://www.ted.com/talks/jill_bolte_taylor_s_powerful_stroke_ of_insight.html

What is particularly interesting is Dr. Taylor's description of her left hemisphere abilities that were diminishing and her right hemisphere functions that remained without the influence of language (see Figure 7.1 for a summary of her left and right hemisphere abilities). She shows us how the left hemisphere is a serial processor, aware of her single separate self, with a record of the past and the future available in linear thinking. The information is available in language and symbols, stored in details, categories, and associations. The past is projected into the future with facts. Here she describes herself as distinct and separate from everyone else: "I am me."

During her stroke, as the left hemisphere functions diminished, Dr. Taylor became aware of the right hemisphere's abilities as a parallel processor that focuses on the present moment. Here her holistic thinking is expressed in images and stored in sensory experience. Here she is one with all, perfect, whole, and connected. The words she uses to share this experience with us are very interesting and reflect her experience of life and the meaning she has created. She uses the word *nirvana* to describe her freedom from mind chatter and years of emotional baggage. The original use of this word is ancient and comes from Hinduism, which describes nirvana as a release from suffering and a union with the Supreme Being, connected to All That Is. As you watch her in the video, you feel the elation and expansiveness of her experience, free from her mind.

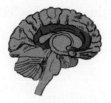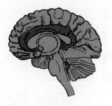

Left Hemisphere

- Serial processor
- Single, separate self
- Record of past and future
- Linear thinking
- Expressed in language
- Storage of: Details
  Categories
  Associations
- Past projected into the future
- Facts
- In process
- Distinct
- Separateness
- I am me

Right Hemisphere

- Parallel processor
- At one with all
- Present moment
- Holistic thinking
- Storage of gestalt with sensory: Smells, tastes, sights, touch, movement, sounds

- Awareness of present
- Energy
- Perfect
- Whole
- Connectedness
- We are one

Explanation by Jill Bolte Taylor

Figure 7.1 Jill Bolte Taylor's right and left hemisphere functions

In neuropsychology, we often use a metaphor to describe the processing of information in the brain: the left hemisphere processes the trees and the right hemisphere processes the forest. In the left hemisphere, we find the details; in the right, the configuration of the details into a whole gestalt. What Jill Bolte Taylor describes is exactly what is described by both neuropsychology and

Siddhartha. Through meditation, rather than a stroke, Siddhartha quieted his mind and found nirvana, enlightenment, and a sense of connection with All That Is.

When Thought Shifts Emotion

When you really catch on to neurochoice—the power to choose your focus and regulate your experience—it is amazing what you see happen. A few years ago, a new patient came in. Hank was a truck driver. He had been injured in a collision and was out of work with a brain injury. He was not happy and not someone who would ever have come into my office if he could have avoided it. For him, this was the spot between the rock and the hard place. He wanted to go back to work and get on the road.

After doing the testing to understand how the injury had affected him, Hank started the biofeedback work to learn to control his emotions, language, and behavior. He was on the verge of burning some bridges he did not want to burn. He also loved his daughter, who was eight years old and loved her daddy. There were motivations in his life to get a handle on what seemed to be justifiable anger and resentment. Those emotions weren't getting him anywhere he wanted to go. After some months of recognizing the sensations of anger in his body and learning the breathing methods, he reached the phase where he could integrate the methods into his life. This is where you want the skills the most, but it can also be the hardest place to use them.

One day Hank was late for group therapy. He came in, apologizing to everyone for the disruption, and explained he had just had a major breakthrough. Hank had planned his time accurately, making an early doctor's appointment, which should have given him plenty of time to get to group. Unfortunately, the doctor was running late and, as Hank sat there in the waiting room, the time ticking by, he realized there was no way he was going to be on time for group. The more he thought about it, the more stressed he got. He could feel his heart racing and muscles tensing. No matter how many times he asked the nurse if something could be done, he was told to wait.

Finally, when Hank was called to go into the examination room to see the doctor, he knew that his blood pressure was elevated and he was ready to say things he would regret. With a flash of insight, Hank asked to use the restroom. He realized that he had to bring his blood pressure down or he would be evaluated for medication he did not want. He used the room as a quiet, private location to close his eyes, breathe, release his muscles, and imagine his peaceful place on the beach. He had learned to slow his heart rate in therapy but had never had to do it like this. Hank had an aversion to medication, which was a powerful motivation to get control of himself.

Hank was a big guy with a big voice and a big laugh. By the time he had finished telling his story in group therapy, he had everyone in the room laughing at the predicament he had been in and the way he had managed to get out of it. The doctor told him his blood pressure was much better than the last visit and that if he could keep it that way he would not need medication. The doctor also asked what it was that Hank was doing to lower his blood pressure. Hank laughed and told him, "Thinking good thoughts." He wasn't ready to discuss just how out of control he had gotten.

Within a matter of minutes, Hank had shifted from raging emotions that had him in and out of his seat in the waiting room to a calm state with a steady heart rate and a good sense of humor. He had learned to recognize body signs—related to his emotions—that created behavior he did not want and now knew what he could do about it. By successfully using his Brain-Body Compass in this way, Hank took advantage of his new theory of mind: he realized that he could shift his emotions by controlling his thoughts.

When you grasp that the glass ceiling is always moving and you can be regulating it moment by moment, you can keep your optimal arousal state readily available instead of hitting the ceiling to find out where it is—and paying the price. A lifestyle where you take care of yourself, eat regularly, sleep well, hydrate often, laugh whenever possible, exercise frequently, and do what you love with those you enjoy will keep the window of the Expansion Zone wide, with lots of resources to use.

The power to regulate thought and choose your focus changes everything. That is why we start there in treatment; everything is easier if that is in place. Thought really does regulate emotion, and once you learn how to do it, you are no longer a prisoner of your own moods and reactions. It is worth the effort to achieve physiological balance through regulation of breath (slowing heart rate and regulating the nervous system) and muscle relaxation through isometric exercises (releasing the physical tension of negative expectation), and to choose positive self-statements in thought (orienting to the solution) for an optimal level of arousal that makes you healthier, happier, and smarter. This is something you can do anytime, anywhere in your daily life. Make the effort to make it a practice, and then it will become automatic when you need it.

When Emotion Shifts Thought

One of the questions I have wondered about is whether the right hemisphere is the localization where we hold the gestalt of the

Expansion Zone. There is a theory that psychotherapy is really an entrainment of the right hemisphere, where unconscious, non-verbal, and emotional information is woven together into self states and self images.[3] In this theory, the therapist serves as a stable bridge to the state the client is reaching for. The therapist envisions a solution to the problem, and as she stays confident in the meaning she has developed, the client's right hemisphere weaves a new awareness of the what and the how of the solution.

It has been enlivening to follow the theories and findings of neuroscience that reveal our inner workings. My own experience is that I must ground myself in a genuine feeling state of my intention for those I am working with in order to fully embody my purpose and keep my focus on it. If I am feeling ambivalent, it will show, and I will be less effective. After working with brain function and brain trauma for thirty years, I can envision a positive outcome for those who come for this information. If I can grasp their desire and make my vision real to them with the certainty of what I have seen, I become the bridge to where they want to go. I must come from the meaning I have learned and manage my own internal state to be consistent with the vision. You can do this as well for your family and friends and anyone you are trying to help. If you are looking at the solution, you can show them the way.

To become this bridge, I get in touch with the Brain-Body Compass by paying attention to information within my body to pick up on physiological information like heart rate, muscle tension, and changes in digestion. Neuroscience now tells us that the subcortical regions like the limbic system and brain stem are able to regulate levels of arousal in the nervous system, thus affecting bodily functions. It also looks like the primary amount of emotional information from the subcortical region comes into the right hemisphere, where it can become a source for shaping the big picture, like a map formed by the cortex. We will see how scientific findings either confirm this current thinking or change it with new discoveries in the future. So far the image works for me to regulate myself.

The effectiveness of the Brain-Body Compass has to do with the meaning you develop in your life. Spirituality and neuro-psychology are major sources of meaning for me. I like to follow new trains of thought that come along in articles, books, and pre-sentations, but continually measure their value against the meaning I have already developed. If it is consistent with what I know of the brain and the body and resonates with me spiritually, I pursue and enjoy the new discoveries and integrate them into my thinking. I'm going with the Dalai Lama's thought: If some-thing comes along that demonstrates that my beliefs are limited, I want to change my beliefs and expand my meaning with the new discoveries. Consider how you develop meaning in your life and how you select new perspectives that offer you growth. You might consider adopting the Dalai Lama's perspective too. If you find this valuable, you may want to focus more often on the sensations in your body during important thoughts and emotions. The more open you are to discovering new sensations and becoming aware of their meaning, the greater power your neurochoice has to regu-late your experience toward your desire.

Awakening Applications

- Be sensitive to your thoughts. Whether or not you go for acupuncture treatments and have experienced needles in your body as a reason for maintaining focus (as I did), you can re-create the same environment at home. While sitting or lying peacefully, focus your mind on an intention. Sustain your intention by noticing the bodily sensations you feel when your intentions waver and other thoughts enter your mind. What effect do those sensations have on your body? Does your chest tighten, your muscles tense, or your breathing become shallow? Observe their effect, and then focus again on your intention. You will know when your focus on your intention has waned when you feel the effect of emotion on your body. Keep coming back to your original intention with focused thought.

• Any form of meditation that releases intrusive thoughts strengthens your cingulate and lets you be more effective in shifting your focus to where you want it. Revisit any of the previous meditation exercises and incorporate them into your daily life.

Notes

1. David Premack and Guy Woodruff. "Does the Chimpanzee Have a Theory of Mind?" *Behavioral and Brain Sciences* 1 (1978) 515–26.

2. John Bowlby, *Separation: Anxiety and Anger* (New York: Basic Books, 1976).

3. Allan Schore, "Right Brain Affect Regulation," *The Healing Power of Emotion*, ed. D. Fosha, J. Siegel, M. Solomon (New York: Norton, 2009), 112–44.

8

A Theory for Seeking Growth and Change

A few years ago, I was teaching for the Maryknoll Sisters renewal program when they shared with me a new theory they were finding helpful called Theory U. They were using it from an organizational perspective for their chapter meeting, where representatives from around the world came together to elect new leadership and formulate a new vision. Theory U is a theory of change that has come out of research at MIT. The Maryknoll Sisters community used it as a guide for the change the whole community was addressing.

THEORY U

Theory U, also referred to as presencing, is a theory developed by Otto Scharmer at MIT.[1] The word *presencing* is a combination of the words *presence* and *sensing*. It represents an active ability to sense, recognize, and act on one's highest future potential. The theory applies to both individuals and groups and demonstrates that the way we attend or focus on something will determine how the situation will unfold.

I have used Theory U in the context of seeking growth and change through personal inner exploration and have found it consistent with my other observations of brain function and psychological and spiritual growth. Figure 8.1 illustrates the steps

The Process of Life's Transitions

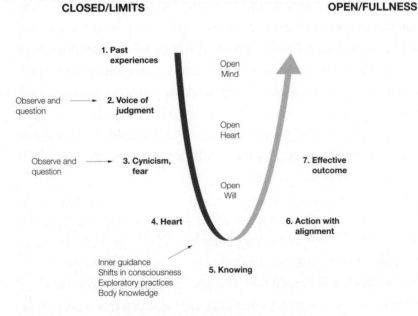

Figure 8.1 The process of life's transitions[2]

described in Theory U for the individual inner journey and gives some names for the places within ourselves that we encounter and come from.

Quite simply, Theory U describes an inner process undertaken to reach a deeper place of certainty and knowing within oneself before acting on an intention. The theory is based on research on highly successful leaders, which was done by interviewing them about their own inner process for decision making. It reminds me of the older spiritual practice of discernment, mentioned in chapter 3, which calls on the deeper wells of spiritual wisdom within each of us.

In Theory U, the intention is to get to a place of certainty within yourself, before you undertake any action, to ensure effectiveness in your efforts. From this place of knowing, your skills are the greatest and your effectiveness is enhanced. The thing is that there are many dimensions of our inner world to traverse before you get there. To me, this sounds similar to arriving deeply in the optimal arousal state, where peak focus, sensitivity, emotional balance, sharpened cognition, rich creativity, and broad awareness await us.

Theory U and the Voice of Judgment

The first stage on the journey to knowing requires getting past what Theory U calls the voice of judgment. This resonates with the chatter of the left hemisphere and old unresolved emotions that can plague us with repeated intrusive thoughts that get in the way of seeing a clear picture of what is going on. Your journey inward will be stopped by having inflexible standards and rules for yourself and others or a habit of being critical. According to

Theory U, getting past the voice of judgment allows you to reach an open mind where broader thinking is possible.

The sisters who were taking this course when we were using Theory U were mostly older, and many were approaching the time when they would stay in the United States and not return to the foreign countries where they had worked and lived. This was a big change, as is any significant alteration in lifestyle or movement into a new phase. When you leave so much behind, it is important to cherish the memories and make peace with the incompletions. Even when you do your best, it doesn't always turn out the way you'd planned. Sharing stories, reflecting on what you learned, and acknowledging what you contributed give you an opportunity to take stock and weave a new story to give your right hemisphere a new perspective. The voice of judgment reflects a lack of acceptance and is a source of suffering. Achieving an open mind gives you access to all your reflective abilities again.

As the sisters and I discussed major life transitions and the brain functions involved at such times, we talked about how every experience strengthens old neural networks or creates new ones and how our powers of intention and focus are the tools to shape that experience. For the nuns, the word *compassion* has both emotional and spiritual meaning, but there was a new definition for the word that fit perfectly for this group. Sister Helen, one of the sisters from the Maryknoll Contemplative Community, had given me a little book by Francis B. Rothluebber called *The Upstart Spring: An Experience in Evolutionary Spirituality*. Rothluebber defines compassion as a fertile ground for change: "Compassion is loving the potential of someone before it comes into being."[3] That is the vision, held in the heart, that can be nurtured into reality. For women, it is often easier to do it for others than to do it for themselves.

With that context, we talked about the voice of judgment, about how to recognize critical thoughts and what to do when they are leading the rest of the orchestra in your brain. Byron Katie has offered some brilliant insights in what she calls "The Work," a method of self-inquiry that she created.[4] She challenges the truth of such critical thoughts and undermines their power, breaking the hold of old neural networks. She had learned that when she believed her thoughts, she suffered, and when she didn't believe them, she didn't suffer. Having the benefit of her insights, we formulated questions about the voice of judgment:

1. What are the most persistent critical thoughts of yourself and others that have surfaced in your life?
2. Can you know these to be true?
3. How have you responded to those thoughts? Have you
   - believed them;
   - argued with them;
   - acted on them;
   - observed them; and/or
   - waited for them to pass?

From this perspective, an observing self begins to see what is happening and has some neurochoice in the matter. With a list of such options, you can see where an approach will get you and whether you want to go there. The nuns are used to reflection; it is an essential skill in the lifestyle. They also know how to sit with an issue and wait for guidance in prayer. This makes sense to them. The more you can observe and disengage from your critical thoughts, the more effective you are with dismantling the automatic neural network that has a grip on you and the stronger your choices become. When you let go of the past perspective you have woven, you will make room for a new one with more effective options. This is how you dismantle a neural network and deconstruct the thought patterns that have shaped your perception of the world.

Theory U and an Open Heart

Next, Theory U guides us to recognize the emotional state and the presence of fear, disappointment, sadness, loss, or any other emotion that holds your thinking in the past. By getting past reluctance, cynicism, and fear, we can come to the place where the truth of the present moment can be felt. Again, we discussed questions to address this inner reality:

1. What are the most persistent fears for yourself and others that have surfaced in your life?
2. What are the reluctant, doubtful, or fearful thoughts that emerge when you consider an impending change?
3. How have you responded to those fears? Have you
    - believed them;
    - argued with them;
    - acted on them;
    - observed them; and/or
    - waited for them to pass?

The key to regulating where you come from and where you will arrive when you act is to recognize the resistance in your emotions and the doubt in your thinking and learn to change the state you are in before you act on an issue.

As we explored the images in my presentation and the group reflected on the concepts, felt the feelings, and considered their intentions, we moved deeper into the process of change. Then we came to the heart—the seat of our emotions and the source of our drive and energy. Here the questions shifted a bit as we reflected on a lifetime, with all its joys and challenges and twists and turns. We discussed the times in life when you need to close your heart as well as the times when you sense the desire to open it:

1. When have you closed your heart to cope with the emotions of your challenges?
2. How are you limited now by the effects of a past need to close your heart?
3. What is your vision of the fullness of emotional experience in the future?
4. What would assist you in achieving that unfolding?
5. What makes your heart sing now?

Everyone in the room had a lot of life experience. Everyone had traveled internationally, lived in other countries and cultures, and made extraordinary adjustments within themselves. Everyone there had spent years exploring and developing an awareness of their inner reality. Yet with all those skills and experiences, many had encountered enormous challenges. Some had seen unspeakable cruelty and suffering. Some had lived under destructive governments and had stayed with the people through revolutions. We talked about how sometimes we must close our heart just to get through an immediate challenge when the pain or horror is beyond what we can bear. What then? How do you open your heart again when you are ready to release the intense emotions that had previously been too much?

This was a very fruitful discussion, and many shared challenges that were beyond my experience and skills. Each spoke of how she had to learn to once again resonate with anything that touched her deeply. One sister who had lived in South America spoke of a time when the military generals were particularly threatening. She recoiled from what they were doing to the innocent indigenous people who lived on the land. She had lived there many years and loved their simplicity. She could not leave them and did not know how to help them. She was between the proverbial rock and hard place—something we can all relate to.

As she told us of her dilemma, she identified with the need to close her heart in the face of the violence she witnessed. Slowly, as she prayed and reflected in nature, she found that achieving a physical resonance with the birds and the sweetness of their songs brought her ease and peace. When she had to consider what to do, she would walk in nature to feel their presence and enjoy their song. She did not use terms like "regulating hyperarousal" to describe her actions, but her spiritual journey had taught her how to do it nonetheless. When she finally achieved a sense of peace by listening to the music of nature, she also found a sense of compassion for the military men who had themselves been trained in cruelty and knew no better. Her experience represented a feeling common to all of us: we sometimes have to step out and get perspective before we can go on.

We asked her how that had helped her and what she had decided to do. She laughed and said that though it may sound silly, she had some socks that had prints of birds woven into them, and she found herself wearing them each day, achieving the alignment and harmony she had found with the birds' songs while walking in nature. She attempted to think with compassion about the generals who were giving these brutal orders and the soldiers who carried out the violence, seeing them as innocent children gone awry. Slowly, she could tolerate opening her heart more and more to the suffering that was happening on all sides. Finally, she told us of her attempts to just talk with these men. She arranged meetings with them that related to her work, but at every opportunity she engaged them in reconnecting with their own hearts. She asked them about their own children. She knew some of their families and discussed encounters with their parents. She spoke to the humanness within them that had to be closed off when they went to work.

As everyone sitting in the circle listened to her story, we all reflected on how we have had to withdraw when life was just too much. There are many who are never able to open the door of their heart again. She was not going to be one of them. After some discussion, I wanted to go back to the story of her time with the generals. I asked her what had helped her be able to walk into the general's office and sit with a person whom it was not safe to be with. How did she stay stable in her intention as she entered the so-called lion's den?

Again, she laughed and said that she had worn the bird-patterned socks to remind her of the birdsong that had opened her heart. When she went to the general's office to talk to him, she had spikes of anxiety and discomfort as she saw and felt what was happening there. When she felt those jabs of reactivity and resistance to her intention, she would look at the bird pattern on her socks and find the feeling of harmony that had set her on this path to assist the general in opening his heart again. By keeping her heart open, she could see, reflected in his eyes, glimmers of his heart opening as well.

This Maryknoll sister did not know about regulating arousal levels in the autonomic nervous system. She knew that if she pushed back against the military, she would no longer be able to help the people she loved. She had learned long ago that staying in a state of Grace blesses those around her, so she brought that state of Grace to the general's office, using compassion to call forth the opening of his heart through the glimmer in his eye. Anyone can use this approach to life—simply choose a symbol that stabilizes your heart, feel it, and focus on it. Some call it regulating the autonomic nervous system; others call it being open to the gift of Grace that is always awaiting you. You choose your own meaning.

Theory U and Open Will

The final step in Theory U is called open will. With an open mind and an open heart, we are finally ready to address the issue or question that requires action. Here we focused on the inner guidance and exploration that leads to shifts in consciousness and bodily knowledge. In Theory U, the term "open will" describes the place within ourselves where we find the Presence of our Higher Self where our deepest KNOWING resides. This represents our highest future possibility, the level of awareness that can allow our potential to actualize. In discussion with the sisters, we looked for the signs of readiness for action and asked more questions:

1. Which emotions—such as curiosity, desire, certainty, or KNOWING—have most guided you in your life choices and been most effective for you?

2. What practices have guided your inner exploration?
3. What are the physical sensations in your body for KNOWING?

Here we talked of the emotions and sensations they recognized as indicators of certainty. The inner guidance they trusted to lead them to the next step is hard to describe, but, as it unfolds, a shift in consciousness happens. There are lots of exploratory practices and bodily knowledge to use to reach the place of KNOWING, enabling action to come from an open will. This is a key distinction. KNOWING, from a place within yourself, when a topic is actionable is the skill of great leaders. When you are coming from that place within yourself, you move past obstacles, focusing on where you are going rather than where you are now. There is no exertion, struggle, or worry. It is more about wondering, appreciating each step, and being able to see how the pieces are coming together.

One of the sisters, who had spent many years in the Contemplative Community in the United States and in foreign countries, came up to me later and said she found it helpful to add the knowledge of the brain functions to her thinking about her inner journey. Although her faith was great and her experience substantial, knowing the actual physical mechanisms made it all the more real to her. She also said she had come across a quote that seemed to fit with the message of my workshop.

The rush and pressure of modern life are a form ... of its innate violence. To allow oneself to be carried away by a multitude of conflicting concerns, to surrender to too many demands, to commit oneself to too many projects, to want to help everyone in everything is to succumb to violence. ... It destroys the fullness of [one's own] work, because it kills the root of inner wisdom which makes the work fruitful.[5]

As I read the quote and thought about its use of the word *violence* to describe life's frenetic pace, I could feel how our world had lost the deep well of inner wisdom, purpose, completion, and satisfaction that so many of the sisters exhibit. How did we get going so fast and lose touch with the deeper reasons for getting up each day? How do we stay in touch with those deeper reasons when the world whirls around us? Theory U is adding to the language of our inner world and our ability to recognize the state we are in.

If you have ever walked through Grand Central Station in New York, surrounded by people who are rushing and running, you realize just how much the environment of the outer world affects the inner world. Suddenly you feel like running too, but you aren't in a hurry. A calm inner state escapes you and steady thoughts start to speed up. Thought shifts emotion and emotion shifts thought. When you seek a deep place of KNOWING within yourself and wait for that feeling and perspective before acting, your thoughts expand beyond the immediate focus created by a feeling of needing to race for the train.

Going from Reacting to Releasing

As a neuropsychologist, I enjoy wondering about the mechanisms of the brain that produce shifts in internal states and alter our perception. What is happening when those critical thoughts of the voice of judgment finally stop criticizing to produce an open mind? What mechanism in the nervous system is facilitating the opening of a threatened, cold, and closed heart? How does the brain orient to a state of KNOWING and grasp the opportunity for action that is assured success?

These are all states with specific, recognizable sensations and emotions. Critical thoughts create an uncomfortable physical and emotional state. The state of an open heart feels different from that of a closed heart. We know the action that comes from an open heart goes in a different direction than the resistant action of a closed heart. But what is the mechanism in the brain that can shift from one to another? And why are some people good at making that shift, while others are not?

When my associate Dr. Jay teaches people methods for managing their stress, he focuses on replacing worrisome thoughts with positive self-statements like "I may be confused and upset right now, but I have figured out complex issues before and with time I will master this one." Next comes regulating the heart rate through rhythmic breathing and releasing muscle tension with isometric exercises. When each step is broken down, we can see how the brain responds to your neurochoice to make you feel better. But can the brain do all this in one step? Some people seem to be able to shift instantly.

How did the Maryknoll sister shift herself from reactive anxiety to focused intentionality while she sat with the general in South America? Somehow her nature walks, where she meditated and enjoyed the sounds of the birds, created a memory of a peaceful, harmonious experience. With practice, she could look at the image of the birds on her socks, return to the memory, and shift her nervous system to be present to their stabilizing influence. She recognized this process as God's Grace available to her because that is the meaning she has developed to access this inner power.

But for those who have not developed such spiritual meaning to recognize these sensations and know how to read them, there is the question about how a meaningful experience can be remembered and valued sufficiently enough to follow. The brain has an ability to recognize meaningful patterns of events and offer you sufficient information to pursue them. Dimensions of synchronicity have been explored in psychology, but we are only just beginning to ask the right questions about these more powerful spiritual abilities that are available to us. My personal experience is that there is a similarity between the interpretation of "the gift of Grace" impacting my life and synchronistic events entering my life. The feeling state is the same for me.

As I wondered about these observations in my life and my patients' lives, another synchronistic experience came along, and because I made a neurochoice to follow the signals my body's compass was putting out, another piece of this puzzle emerged. On the trip to Alaska I had taken before I met Kathy on the train to Portland, I kept running into two young women, Stephanie and Nancy, who were also on the same cruise. They were bright, fun, attractive young women and, with a series of chance encounters, we had many great conversations. Later I found them behind me in line to be seated for dinner, so I had the pleasure of dining with them as well. When the universe delivers these chance encounters, I typically feel the lights go on inside. There is something curious and fun that gets my interest. It feels like a yes! When you're looking for an answer, a synchronistic event will often provide it if you're awake to it coming to you.

During dinner, the conversation turned to health and healing practices, and they told me of a Kundalini yoga teacher with whom they were studying, Mimi Trotter, who also taught Sat Nam

Rasayan. This was something I had never heard of, but I'm attracted to anything described as a meditation for physical healing. On returning home, I arranged to talk to Mimi. Sure enough, lots of synchronistic connections kept surfacing. Mimi had gone to a high school in Hawaii run by the Maryknoll Sisters. She knew lots of these lovely women, some of whom I knew as well.

Under Mimi's guidance, I started to learn the meditation Sat Nam Rasayan, which means "Deep Relaxation in the Divine Name." My experience of the meditation is that it trains you in directing your consciousness toward an awareness of your body in order to perceive what is felt there, because the healing knowledge is manifested through the physical sensation. Allowing yourself to feel the physical sensation is the first step to enabling your awareness to release the sensation. In Sat Nam Rasayan, the only healing method is your consciousness and its influence on physical sensation.

I started learning this healing method from Mimi but was also aware that it is best grasped through feeling the sensations. I knew I would catch on more easily if I were in a class where others were creating an environment where it could be felt. Three weeks later I was on a weeklong retreat with Guru Dev, who learned this healing method, which is handed down through an ancient lineage, from Yogi Bhajan. Guru Dev went on to write the book *Sat Nam Rasayan: The Art of Healing,* which for the first time put language to an art that for centuries had been taught in silence through sensation.[6]

Thanks to Mimi, I managed to get to the retreat, learn to sit on the floor with a back support (this was a stretch for me, literally—my hips just won't stay in a cross-legged position for long), and focus on my body sensations. Being aware of all your body sensations at once is the first step. Then you learn to use the power of your intention to release the physical tensions and achieve an open ease. This state is called the "sensitive space," where you are aware of all the body sensations at once and are able to do something about those unwanted sensations.

After you find the sensitive space, the next step is to recognize that all these sensations are equally important and sacred. By holding all the sensations as sacred, you move into the process of releasing resistance to the well-being that awaits you. This is considered entering your Sacred Space. This dimension of the meditation practice is about learning to enter the healing consciousness of the Sacred Space and enable change for the greater ease and wellness of yourself or another.

These are the basic skills. When we mastered them, we began inviting an awareness of the physical sensations that arise in us due to the presence of another we are focusing on. People worked as partners, focusing on each other. By reaching your Sacred Space and then touching your partner, new sensations arise. You become aware of sensations related to them that are different from your own sensations. In releasing these sensations that you have allowed in, you release them in the other person as well.

For many years, I have worked with people struggling with trauma and have felt their struggle myself. The ability to meditate and release those sensations for both them and myself is extremely appealing. When someone is facing a challenge, they usually talk about the symptoms of the injury and the effects to be overcome, wanting to get back to where they were and to what they had known and done. It sounds too simple—the idea that by focusing on the problem we are resisting a well-being that awaits us—but simple answers are usually the most effective.

After reading Guru Dev's book and talking with Mimi about how this works, the meditation became a part of my practice. Commonly I will meditate with a patient who is in distress for about fifteen minutes at the beginning of the session. This way, our discussions are more focused and fruitful. Patients report being more grounded and productive in the session, and I observe less hyperarousal reactivity as we discuss the difficult challenges they face. My ability to be aware of the sensations in my body while I am with them and to release them in the meditation puts us both in a higher playing field for the conversation. Treatment goes much faster from that state.

Although it sounds abstract, it is wonderful to get past your own voice of judgment, open your heart, and step into a confidence that all will be well. However, getting to the starting line is always the challenge. The key is "allowing," which means letting the challenge be what it is, free of judgment, worry, or reaction. Allowing resistances after entering your Sacred Space enables you to release them so that they disappear.

Is this ancient healing art how Jesus and other healers in history influenced the well-being of so many? They restored physical, emotional, and cognitive well-being to believers who came to them. Perhaps Sat Nam Rasayan is an integration of Dr. Jay's three steps of replacing the thought; regulating the breath, heart, and nervous system; and releasing the physical tension. Is that what we mean when we talk about "releasing resistance"? Is that what the sister from South America was doing when she looked at her bird-patterned socks so that she could keep her heart open and not orient to the general whom so many feared?

My message is that there are many paths to achieving this kind of growth and change. With an awakened brain, you can be open to synchronistic events, symbols, and body sensations that will guide you to the methods and teachers you seek. You will find what works for you if you are open to it. Recognizing, replacing, regulating, and releasing, all in one step—that is what an awakened brain can do.

Awakening Applications

• Try out Theory U for yourself. The idea behind Theory U helps you get to a place of certainty within yourself, before you undertake any action, to ensure your effectiveness. From this place called KNOWING, your skills are the greatest. Go back to the questions I discussed with the Maryknoll sisters (beginning on p. 193) and apply them to your own life. Feel free to write the answers in your journal and let your thoughts flow.

• How do you soothe yourself from stressful feelings? Take a tip from the Maryknoll sister who found solace from her special socks: Find an image or object that has significance to you and make it easily accessible to you in times of stress. Perhaps it's a piece of jewelry, an item you keep in your pocket, or an image your mind can focus on when you close your eyes. Find what speaks to you and keep it handy so that you can easily shift yourself from reactive anxiety to focused intention.

Notes

1. C. Otto Scharmer, *Theory U* (Cambridge, MA: Theory U Society for Organizational Learning, 2007).

2. C. Otto Scharmer, *Presence in Action: An Introduction to Theory U* (Vienna, Austria: Society for Organizational Learning Forum, 2005).

3. Francis B. Rothluebber, *The Upstart Spring: An Experience in Evolutionary Spirituality* (Idyllwild, CA: Colombiere Center, 2005), 83.

4. Byron Katie, *Loving What Is: Four Questions That Can Change Your Life* (New York: Harmony Books, 2002).

5. Thomas Merton, *Conjectures of a Guilty Bystander* (New York: Image Books, 1968), 81.

6. Guru Dev Singh, *Sat Nam Rasayan: The Art of Healing* (Rome, Italy: Edizioni e/o, 2009).

9

The Power of Belief:
The Inner World Creates
the Outer World

How did the three stonecutters we talked about in chapter 2 get to where they were? They were all in the same physical place, cutting the same stones, but each of them was coming from a very different place within themselves. Each was having a very different experience of the same job. How did this come to be? Maybe you know people who are like one of them. Maybe you are like one of them. Maybe at different times in your life you have been like each of them.

Each of these men had had very different life experiences that had led them to the point of expressing different meanings about the same job. Life experiences and our daily choices about the meaning they have build a set of interpretations in the brain, which then becomes their meaning for us. Whatever meaning we have created, day by day, will color our perceptions of later events and infuse the meaning we then bring to new experiences. We can observe and consciously consider our experience and our choices, or we can just react, believing each sensation of emotion; either way, we are building the neural network that will produce our next perception of similar events. Based on how we construct the inner room of our experience and the way we furnish it, we can live in an inner jail, an inner home, or an inner cathedral just like the three stonecutters. My early years in the novitiate were focused on learning to bring an awareness of the sacred to my work in the kitchen, the laundry, the sewing room, and the garden. I would not have said it this way then, but I was learning to create my own meaning by staying silent all day as I worked and paid more attention to my inner world than my outer world.

Belief Begins with the Creation of Meaning

When I think of those who have created such meaning in their lives, I immediately think of Mother Teresa. She had an experience in which she perceived that Jesus was calling her to assist the poor. This experience was so strong for her that she founded a religious community, the Missionaries of Charity in Calcutta, India, in 1950. Here, she and those who joined her ministered to the poor, sick, orphaned, and dying. Her inner reality—that Jesus had called her to alleviate the suffering of the poor—brought her to international awareness, which continues to inspire millions of people. She was given the Nobel Peace Prize for living the reality she perceived. In her lifetime, her work developed 610 missions in 123 of the 195 countries in the world. She died in 1997, but others continue to align with her vision so that it continues today.

Mother Teresa was influenced at a young age by St. Thérèse of Lisieux, whose mystical spirituality was oriented to simplicity. The creation of meaning starts very young, and many of us make decisions in childhood that guide us through our whole lives. We may not realize that our body is a compass or that we have chosen a North Star to follow, but those early experiences stay with us. When Mother Teresa was asked for advice on how to handle a conflict, she always said the same thing: Pray first before acting and you will be guided. When I watch her in interviews, she says this repeatedly to people who ask about challenges in relationships and how to make a decision. I wonder what it was like for her to "pray first" and where it took her within herself to undertake her next step. She took many steps, living from the meaning she chose to follow and creating a better world. She acknowledged she was not always in touch with her inspiration, but she continually chose to return to it. Mother Teresa believed Jesus had called her to do this work, even on days when she wasn't feeling the same inspiration she had when that experience first happened. Her belief in what was possible for the poor and suffering, combined with the meaning she had developed and sustained, had an impact on our world that few people ever have. Mother Teresa chose to find God in those who were suffering, and that belief sustained her.

St. Thérèse of Lisieux

St. Thérèse of Lisieux (1873–97) was a Carmelite nun who was known for her love of simplicity. From a young age she desired to do all things well with confidence and love. She was called Little Flower because of the meaning she had embraced in life. Her determination to find God in all the little kindnesses and caring acts distinguished her desire for authenticity and alertness to the sacred in all things. She faced ill health all her life and died at twenty-four years of age, but within these challenges, she found the depth of meaning she sought:

> Instead of becoming discouraged, I said to myself: God cannot inspire unrealizable desires. I can, then, in spite of my littleness, aspire to holiness. It is impossible for me to grow up and so I must bear with myself such as I am with all my imperfections. But I want to seek out a means of going to heaven by a little way, a way that is very straight, very short, and totally new.[1]

Mother Teresa's practice of praying first resonates with Theory U and the value of acting only after you have shifted to an inner place beyond judgment and fear. There is a certainty in how Mother Teresa spoke when asked for advice. If you watch footage of her discussing her life and her vision, you can see that she spoke from the deeply strengthening meaning she'd developed. See what it feels like to you. The saints live on on YouTube.

Mother Teresa discusses her life and vision.
http://www.youtube.com/watch?v=u-3gDwk178E&feature=related

Was Mother Teresa's brain affected by her early experiences? I can't see how it could not have been. Is spiritual inspiration just a matter of activating neurons? I don't think so. Each of her experiences shaped who she became and shaped her brain to see the world with a deep belief and a passion for alleviating suffering. The meaning she chose focused her on opportunities that repeatedly reinforced the neural network of the belief through which she saw the world.

But what about the people I work with whose brain injuries have changed their perception of the world? I think of this often and consider it when I meet with clients. Jill Bolte Taylor, in relating her experience of her left hemisphere stroke, tells us of the unfolding of the meaning that came to her from that clearly unwanted experience. She obviously makes it sound easier than it is. A brain injury is no picnic. Nonetheless, numerous people have told me that if they had to do it over again, they would still do the brain injury; they had grown that much. At times it is hard to believe. And at other times, when the big picture is available to you, you know these challenges are what bring forth the strength within us.

Taylor tells us of the expansiveness of her experience of nirvana— free from the chatter of her mind and profoundly connected with All That Is. This experience gave her a reason and purpose to get better, because she had an idea worth sharing. She created her own meaning in that life-threatening event and lives from joy as a result. Watch her again in the video in chapter 7 and see how it feels to you. What is the compass of your body saying to your brain as you listen to her experience?

In her presentation, she tells us of euphoria, of feeling like a genie liberated from her bottle. She had found nirvana—and if she had found nirvana while she was still alive, everyone can find nirvana. Throughout her talk, she continually invites us to "step to the right of your left hemisphere and run that deep inner peace circuitry within you." That is definitely a neuroanatomist's description of the rich depth and calm that comes over the body during meditation when the left hemisphere stops talking. It reminds me of Desmond Tutu's wordless prayer, which he describes as feeling like he is sitting next to a warm stove on a cold day.

Taylor's words perfectly describe what I think of as being deeply within the Expansion Zone of optimal arousal in the autonomic nervous system. That is why she calls it "deep inner peace circuitry." The body is filled with circuitry that conveys electrical charges that are determined by the thoughts (or lack thereof) in the brain. Taylor describes you and me as the Life Force Power of the Universe with two cognitive minds and the power to choose how we want to be. Then she asks you, which do you choose? If you watch her and are open to the meaning she has created, consider answering her question for yourself. Which of your cognitive minds and which of your arousal states do you choose to come from in your life?

Finally, I'd like to consider the meaning created by Father Bede Griffiths, who also experienced a left hemisphere stroke and was able to share his experience of spiritual growth that came from it. His description was quite different from Taylor's on some levels and very much the same on others.

Although Father Griffiths described his stroke as a medical condition that caused him to think that he was going to die, mostly he conveyed a spiritual joy and expansion of consciousness similar to those expressed by Taylor. Griffiths spent his life in an ashram in India, but he was a British Benedictine monk, a student and friend of C. S. Lewis, and an ordained priest. However, during his life in India, he wrote extensively on the Hindu-Christian perspective and lived the Christian ashram lifestyle. Because of this integration of traditions, Griffiths became a proponent of what is called integral thought, an attempt to integrate different dimensions of thought, including science and spirituality, for a new theology.

From Father Griffiths's perspective, his left hemisphere stroke and the changes in his brain that resulted were a "death of the mind." This comes from the meaning he had created over the course of his life in his spiritual practice and publications, which were influenced by Christianity and Hinduism. He said that after his stroke he felt a need to "spiritually surrender to the Mother," which overwhelmed him with love. Here he is referring to a quality in his experience that is deeply loving, intimate, and feminine. He believed in a loving God and felt a change in himself consistent with the meaning through which he perceived the world. When you hear him talk on YouTube (http://www.youtube.com/watch?v=wOAlyl 7u2dw), you know you are not listening to a neuroanatomist. You hear the language of his spiritual meaning as he describes feeling an openness to the Divine Feminine and a death of his dualistic mind, which refers to a perception of being separate from that which is the Sacred. He says he is now always aware that there is something more beyond anything he sees, referring to that ineffable sense of being one with the Sacred. He views Love as the basis of his experience, which other perceptions have previously obscured. He describes death as the experience of being taken into Total Love, and speaks of surrendering to Love as he describes the insight he has gained from this experience. His view of death varies from the fear many others experience because of the meaning he has created during his life.

What does it feel like to watch Mother Teresa, Jill Bolte Taylor, and Father Bede Griffiths describe the meaning they have created in their lives and how it shapes their perceptions of the world? Don't be limited by their words; rather, feel what it means to them. There are many ways to describe sensations in the body in relation to the context of the experience. Read the compass of your own body and identify the feeling of the message and the messenger. Commonly, the seeming contradiction—a joyful embrace of death—is met by shock, puzzlement, relief, inspiration, liberation, and/or expansion, depending on the meaning life and death have for you. With an awareness of those sensations, focus on your own meaning. Doing this helps you to get past the reactivity to the differences that are found in our use of language, cultural expression, and belief systems about life and death. We all use somewhat different language for our experiences, but we are all creating meaning for a purpose. Focus on how it feels. Use the guidance of your Brain-Body Compass and then reach for the meaning that is there for you.

The Inner World Creates the Outer World

Mother Teresa, Jill Bolte Taylor, and Father Bede Griffiths are people who created meaning in their lives and brought that meaning to what they did by using it to interpret life's most challenging experiences. They even managed to find joy and inspiration in the most painful, life-threatening experiences. They created a meaning from these big experiences, which shaped how they saw the world and how they functioned in it. Their inner worlds influenced how they perceived their outer world, enabling them to function on a completely different level than most of us. Each of them decided on the conductor of their orchestra. They built a body of thought and made choices about how they thought and acted every day. When they were met by experiences that would overwhelm most of us, the meaning was there to guide them to sing a tune that grounded them in optimal arousal and could move them forward to an expanded level of awareness.

The state you choose to return to every day will determine the skills available to you and the eyes with which you see your journey. The quality of the daily journey you experience comes from the conditioning of your autonomic nervous system and the cognitive thoughts you have identified with. People have strokes every day, and many of them come into my office. Those who have belief in something to call on and have created meaning in their lives seem to do the best. But that is true of everyone in everything. As Mother Teresa advised, if we "pray first" before acting—whatever that means to you and wherever you go within yourself—there is a KNOWING available to us all.

As American poet Philip Booth wisely wrote: "How you get there, is where you'll arrive."[2] Each "tune you sing"—the ways you interpret meaning in your life events—will take you to a different inner room to live in and give a very different perception of life. Your thoughts set the tone for your nervous system's level of arousal and shape your perceptions. Jill Bolte Taylor is actually calling us to tune the instrument of our bodies by "running the deep inner peace circuitry" within us, which is the effect of daily meditation. Strengthening your belief with practices like meditation, journaling, or spiritual direction shapes your brain's capacity to interpret perception of sensory stimulation by focusing your eyes on the meaning you have created.

The three stonecutters all perceive their work from the meaning they have created about what they are doing. From that creation of meaning comes the deeper resonant experience for their beliefs about life events. Even the latter two, who have respectively created an inner home and an inner cathedral and are able to experience that meaning and describe it can likewise lose their grounding in that KNOWING when the world presents them with challenges. We can all lose our balance at times. I have faced disillusionment many times when people have been critical of my efforts or unappreciative when I have given my best. The powerlessness of disillusionment can either derail me or be an opportunity to expand in areas I had not previously encountered. How I choose to view it—as an opportunity, challenge, or threat— is up to me. I have learned that my growing edge, or opportunity to expand, will always be there to be encountered; no matter where I go, it will come up.

People often expect that those living in an intentional community or religious life do not encounter the daily frustrations and challenges that throw you off and require you to dig deeper within yourself. My friend Sister Pat was asked about this in a seminar we attended together. She smiled at the notion of being free of frustration and conflict and explained that even if some of life's challenges are removed in a monastic lifestyle, there is always something to disturb the peace and cause you to choose once again. It might be as simple as what is served for dinner or how someone else speaks or acts. As St. Benedict said when asked about what they do in the monastery, "We fall and get up, fall and get up, fall and get up."

The Neuropsychology of Processing Beliefs

It is a common occurrence for people to have spiritual experiences, struggle to understand them, and then find the meaning in them later. In my own life, after I left the convent, a desire to explore and read about the inner world led me to a book that intrigued me. It is called *Diving Deep and Surfacing* by Carol Christ, and it is about women's spiritual experiences, often in nature.[3] The title has always stayed with me as a perfect description of this inner journey of creating meaning and accessing it. We dive deeply within ourselves, but then we must read the message and return with a new perspective. That is what creative reflection is all about. Recognizing where you want to come from and knowing how to get there when you lose your way is the skill of the awakened brain.

This brings us back to the frontal lobes, where working memory resides (see Figures 3.2 and 3.3 in chapter 3). When Mother Teresa prayed first before she spoke, she was making a choice to use her working memory and manipulate her immediate thought in mind to put it in a context of meaning she had chosen to live by. She spent years "running the deep inner peace circuitry" within herself, using prayer and ritual with her community to ground herself in a reality she perceived. Hers was a spirituality of action. Did this habit of "praying first" before acting bring her to KNOWING? I have not studied her writings to know much of her inner experience, but I do see what she has to say about her purpose and what came out of her efforts. When you take the time to connect to your deepest meaning and believe you can act effectively from that perspective, you will find the way. Somehow she found a place within herself that gave her a passion for alleviating suffering in the world. Whatever she felt as she moved forward from there, there was obviously a power available to her when she focused on her intention and lived from the vision she chose to hold in mind.

Spiritual practice can be a kind of pre-paving for later experience. We know from sports psychology that the brain can be primed for later manifestation of an experience like pre-paving the road you will go down. When I think about this, I ask myself, what am I paying attention to? I can also control my attention, right down to interrupting my thoughts. I learned that the hard way—when I was on the acupuncture table—but I gave myself relief from coughing by changing my focus of thought. Do I want to focus on the inner world where I have some choice in how I feel and how I will act? Do I want to turn to the outer world for input? At any time, I can shift my attention, which will alter my emotion. The power of the frontal lobes—the power of neurochoice—is being able to observe the information coming from your Brain-Body Compass and consider your options. When you have decided on your North Star and spent time resonating with how that feels, your compass will guide you to your heart's desire.

In the Buddhist scripture, Vimalakirti Sutra, they say that "reality is perceived through your own body."[4] Your choice of focus, which creates your inner reality, is the strongest tool you have. Employing both meditation and imagination grounds you in the feeling that your intention is stronger than your reaction. You regulate your autonomic nervous system with your focus and the ways you live to strengthen it.

Figure 9.1, "Coming from Meaning," illustrates my current thinking about my bodily experience of living from meaning, which you can apply to your own life. As shown from bottom to top in the illustration, the bodily state is the source of information for the present experience. This is where, within the body, the needle of the compass points to what is happening. This is where chemical and vibrational information reside. Our cells are made

Coming from Meaning

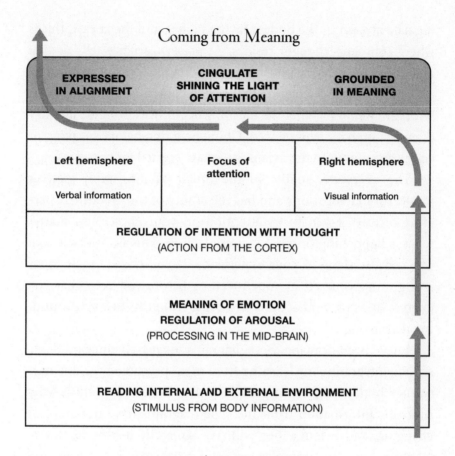

EXPRESSED IN ALIGNMENT	CINGULATE SHINING THE LIGHT OF ATTENTION	GROUNDED IN MEANING
Left hemisphere ———— Verbal information	Focus of attention	Right hemisphere ———— Visual information

REGULATION OF INTENTION WITH THOUGHT
(ACTION FROM THE CORTEX)

MEANING OF EMOTION
REGULATION OF AROUSAL
(PROCESSING IN THE MID-BRAIN)

READING INTERNAL AND EXTERNAL ENVIRONMENT
(STIMULUS FROM BODY INFORMATION)

Figure 9.1 Coming from meaning[5]

up of chemicals, and the cells' surfaces vibrate to activate the chemistry, creating different sensations. Your sensations are a manifestation of your internal state, which is responding to your focus on both internal and external experience.

Moving up the illustration, the nervous system brings information to the regions of your mid-brain, like the brain stem and the limbic system, which are now thought to have the capacity to regulate arousal in the body. Moving higher into the cortex, this is where conscious thought resides. At present, science tells us that emotional and sensory information first registers in the right hemisphere, where the big picture of the present moment resides. This is where we weave together the meaning of our lives from the tapestry of events we have experienced. Going here first before speaking or acting grounds us in the meaning we have created for ourselves.

The cingulate, solidly in the center of the brain, receives input from all locations and has the ability of the executive operating officer; it can focus attention on your choice, no matter what is happening or what you are feeling. This is a muscle that can run the show of your experience. If you choose your focus and ground yourself in your meaning before you act, what you express in words and actions will come from this deeper grounding within you.

I have been drawing these diagrams for myself since graduate school, integrating my learning from neuropsychology and neuroscience both for my own growth and to better serve those who seek this information from me. The diagrams have not stopped changing, and I doubt they will. We are really in the infancy of learning how this complex array of parts works together and how we can better maximize their potential. This illustration can help you consider the many dimensions of your experience and resonate with the belief in your ability to manage your own experience, because you have a map to guide you.

Living from a Vision in the Frontal Lobe

One of my own most powerful experiences of the richness available from the meaning I have created and the beliefs that have sustained me when I have embarked on new challenges came with writing this book. As I prepared to write, the hours and days I had designated for writing instead became filled with one obstacle after the next. Finally, I contacted my friends at Maryknoll and asked if I could visit for the weekend so that I could actually begin. On Friday afternoon, my friend Sister Genie Lorio and I explored the building for a quiet spot and came to a large room with a high ceiling, windows, and entrances to a bedroom and bath. Immediately I felt the strong, deep peace of this place and felt calm and comfortable there. The room had only a few pieces of furniture: a large desk with a chair and a long table with ten chairs around it. As it turned out, this had been the office of the foundress of the Maryknoll Sisters. Mollie Rogers, or Mother Mary Joseph, was most present in her bedroom and office suite, with pictures on the walls, artifacts, and journals available for viewing. This was the perfect place to begin.

Not yet knowing how I would piece together all these bits of experience, insight, and knowledge, I laid out my materials and filled the long table. As I came to the corner of the table at the far end, an attached note simply stated, "Council Meeting Table from Rosary House. Made by Brother Albert, MM." This was the council table where the leadership of the Maryknoll sisters, fathers, and brothers had sat to envision and create this great community. As I comprehended the creative energy that surrounded this table for one hundred years, a simple, humbling awareness came over me, and I knew this was the perfect place for my small contribution to begin to take shape.

For almost a year I had been developing ideas for a book, but clinical and teaching schedules made the power of focus elusive. Here in this place, finally, my left hemisphere could start putting down on paper the bits of information that had been accumulating there for decades. Finally, my right hemisphere could begin to see the shape of a story I had dreamed into existence in my life travels, and it was happily knitting, knitting, knitting together the pieces.

That afternoon, as I began to shape the chapters, concepts, stories, and relationships between the inner and outer world, an unsure physical tension left me and peace emerged. It was as though my left hemisphere had been overloaded with bits and pieces and the driving tension to draw the map that those pieces could become was moving me forward. The brain is happiest and most at peace when the vision is clear and the map is in hand to guide the journey. My map was beginning to emerge from all the pieces laid out on the council table, and an inner peace was returning, born from an erupting, driven energy that insisted on making sense of all the facts and discoveries that cluttered my thoughts.

With my map taking shape and a peaceful enthusiasm starting to emerge, I was better able to take in the support of my loving friends. The richness of a supportive community is hard to describe and contains a power like no other. The sense of being connected to others and supported by them expands the optimal arousal state for the brain to think beyond where it would normally go. The gifts came when I least expected them. One friend, Sister Rita, stopped in the hallway to inquire about my progress and listened attentively to my process of organizing all the material on the council table. To her, it brought to mind the idea of building the scaffold to work from, and she suggested that I look out the window by the elevator to see the amazing construction scaffold that had been erected on the back side of the center building to repair the brick facing. Piece upon piece, the scaffold rose five floors and enabled the workmen to travel smoothly from one end of the building to the next. I enjoyed looking out the window at the scaffold, and I walked outside to firmly establish a snapshot in my mind.

Isn't this exactly what we are doing when the right hemisphere knits together the bits and pieces of our lives to tell the story? Isn't this exactly what those little neurons are doing when they reach out and connect to one another for the first time, lighting up the aha within us? The brain and the neural networks that process our perceptions to create our experience are the scaffold that we build by deciding on the meaning we will give to our lives. Neuroplasticity is the neurological mechanism for connecting the dots, arriving at the aha, because you have configured the forest as you chose to see it. Knitting, knitting, knitting will happen by choice or by chance, so do yourself a favor and choose. I chose to move forward to build my own scaffold on the council table, in my brain and in my computer.

When you recognize a desire to do something meaningful but you are compromised by tension and a lack of certainty, you move forward more slowly. When you have the support and encouragement of others and your own progress serves as evidence for your belief that you can fulfill your goal, a sense of confidence builds within you, and your ease and productivity expand. As you continue to read my story of this process, consider your own experiences of the power of your belief in what is possible for you.

Feeling peace and stability from the scaffolding I had built, I visited Maryknoll again the following weekend—this time to write. As I returned to the left hemisphere, but now with the guidance of the right, one thought enhanced the next and I knew I was ready to begin. At the council table, I took out my computer and long extension cord to reach across the room to the outlet, only to discover that the cord was too short. But this minor inconvenience yielded a great gift: I had to move to Mollie's desk, with its long and wide surface, upon which sat four volumes of her journal, held by bookends inscribed with the words "Who Sendeth Knowledge as the Light."

As I sat down, I took a deep breath and looked up to see a whole new view of the room. I felt a sense of spaciousness that invited my thoughts to come forward. With deep appreciation, I thanked her and all these hundreds of beautiful women who had responded to her invitation first expressed back in 1912, which created this magical room and this dynamic community.

With that, I began to write about the wonders of the ever-awakening brain, that amazing organ in our heads that processes our physical experience and adapts to our requests and choices. Smoothly and easily, the words flowed from my brain to my fingers and onto my laptop screen. As I described the frontal lobe functions of working memory, focus of attention, and the capacity to create an intention or vision, I paused to think about the autonomic nervous system and the visceral organs that, when activated, make our thoughts so real in the body. I glanced up from the computer to consider the connections in this information highway within us and, looking across the council table, I saw on the wall a picture that I had not noticed before. In my effort to get my thoughts out on the table (literally), I had not taken in the image. There, looking at me, was Mary Josephine (Mollie) Rogers and the first group of women who had joined her as secretaries to begin realizing their vision, their dream of bringing services to foreign lands. Staring back at me were seven women with their long hair pinned up on the top of their heads and dressed in the style of the early 1900s with lace collars high around the neck (see Figure 9.2).

Figure 9.2 The first seven Maryknoll secretaries who came in 1912 to offer clerical services. Front row, L–R: Mary Louise Wholean, Anna Maria Towle, Mary Josephine (Mollie) Rogers, Sara Sullivan. Back row, L–R: Mary Augustine Dwyer, Nora Shea, Margaret Shea

Used with permission. Maryknoll Sisters Photo Library.

If I had any doubt remaining that a thought, a dream, a vision can create reality, it left me at that moment. These seven women had come together with a vision they shared, believed, and KNEW was unfolding. They had not intended to become nuns. They were drawn to this new idea of contributing to others in foreign lands (decades before the Peace Corps existed). Together they began living from an intention, which, at times over the years, some thought impossible. But they persisted through each and every obstacle, including the Great Depression. The spirit of their vision has called forth 3,498 women who have gone to forty countries or territories in these one hundred years. Their efforts built this international center and numerous schools, hospitals, and other institutions around the world that have, over time, been given to the people of the culture. Their effort, and that of all those who came to follow them, created realities all over the world. And they started from nothing but a vision.

With that awareness in mind, I continued to write about this amazing organ, the brain, which can dream reality into existence. Mollie has been one example to me of someone who successfully manifested a vision. I encourage you to think of a figure in your own life or experience who has brought into reality a creation that is meaningful for you. Think of that person when you are working to achieve your own vision, and you will find the inspiration to keep going.

How Belief Manifests a Creation

Certainly Mollie Rogers is among many others whose beliefs manifested a creation well beyond their initial vision. As a college student, she saw young women of Protestant faiths going on missions to foreign lands, and wanted to make that opportunity available within her religion as well. She did not think she was founding a religious community (see Figure 9.3). At the beginning of such an undertaking, you have no idea where it will take you, but trusting the process and being willing to follow it are really all you need.

Mollie was willing to view life from what I call pilgrim eyes, as I described in chapter 4. She is often quoted as saying, "Let us go forth and see what God has in store for us." She was open to being

Figure 9.3 Photo of Mary Josephine (Mollie) Rogers, taken two days before coming to Maryknoll, September 1912

Used with permission. Maryknoll Sisters Photo Library.

guided to her next step. She let life unfold from belief, and the community continues to do the same. What I have always loved about Maryknoll sisters is that they are adventuresome women, open to finding the spirit in all peoples, cultures, languages, and customs. They are women who serve around the world in refugee work; medical, educational, and ecological work; leadership training; and promotion of women's causes. They consistently reevaluate their mission and chart a new course for the times they are in. This is not easy for hundreds of women, spread around the world, to do in the Catholic Church.

In the Catholic tradition, each religious community is considered to have its own unique charism, which is defined as a unique spirit considered a "gift of Grace" and based on the founder's intention and the spiritual path originally developed in the community. This is considered to be a power whose source is the Holy Spirit. Each community is considered to have different gifts, according to the charism given to them for the purpose of their service or ministry. It is believed to be a gift freely given by God for spiritual ability and manifestation of their purpose in the world.

The charism of the Maryknoll Sisters followed the tradition founded by St. Dominic described as "contemplation in action." Mother Mary Joseph is often quoted as saying, in regard to a Maryknoll sister, "I would have her distinguished by the saving grace of a sense of humor," and that they have (see Figure 9.4). "Joy is the infallible sign of the presence of God," and I always find it at Maryknoll.[6] Another defining characteristic, as Mollie identified in the charism, is "a worldwide unprejudiced heart." That is a spirit I, too, aspire to and reach for when I have lost my way. Those who knew Mollie are still telling the stories of their encounters with her. When you hear the story of their conversations, there is always a sense of her total presence to the person in the moment. She had an interest in each sister's experience and who they were. That certainly is stepping to the right of your left hemisphere and coming from "a worldwide unprejudiced heart."

Mollie lights the way for the Maryknoll Sisters and others who believe in focusing on what is possible. Mother Teresa followed the charism of St. Thérèse of Lisieux as a guide on her path. All these women spent their lives steeped in developing a meaning that sustained them and believed that Grace was always available to them. They were influential in the world because the development of that meaning guided them in their thinking and enabled them to believe that they could accomplish something that others did not.

Figure 9.4 Mother Mary Joseph, MM, founder of the Maryknoll Missionary Sisters, at her desk at the Motherhouse in New York, 1940

Used with permission. Maryknoll Sisters Photo Library.

We all need such figures to guide the way—those who have gone before us who can ring our bell and give us something to resonate with in our own unique way to fulfill our reason for being here. Religions have been doing this for thousands of years. At times religion loses its way and more emphasis is placed on the institution and the outer world than the spiritual development of the person and the inner world. All large groups occasionally go out of balance and need a correction to get back on a more meaningful path.

I really appreciate that this is an age in history when people are learning to follow their own "felt sense" within them instead of the rules provided from outside by religion, government, education, and business institutions. That is why I have written this book. I have gone through phases when I was angry at the Catholic Church for its mistakes and slowness to change. It was a time when I was young and more reactive to what I did not want than secure in KNOWING and living what I did want. The more I have followed my own bliss, defined my own meaning, found a place in the world that fits me, and grounded myself in my own purpose, the more accepting I have become of this very flawed world. In fact, I've grown to appreciate the flaws as the impetus for growth. I have reactions that are not calm and kind. But that has now become my fertile ground for growth. Whether it is a person, religion, government, or business, their mistakes—just as much as their inspiration—are there to guide us to our potential.

When it comes to religion, the human limitations are all there too. I know of no groups that have formed to share spiritual meaning that don't have their problems. I admire how far Catholicism has come despite its problems and rigidity. As I have grown and faced my own challenges, I can appreciate more of the Church's. Now I can appreciate that Catholics are a group that has spread around the world and inspired people to feed, clothe, educate, heal, and help more people than any other single organization I have ever seen. It is up to me to find those who share the meanings that inspire my growth and allow others to do the same. The things that were meaningful to me twenty years ago have changed, and I expect my perspective to keep changing as I grow and learn. No two brains are the same, and they never will be. I look for those who inspire me, and I encourage you to do the same.

I recently spoke to a woman from Ireland who told me that there is a movement away from the Catholic Church there. She said the book *The Secret,* which is about creating your life as you want it by aligning with and living from your intention, had become very popular because people had developed such a mentality of following the outer reality of rules given to them by the

Church that they had not incorporated the essential message of Love as independently meaningful. She said the essential message of following your own conscience, a central theme of *The Secret,* was discouraged because the authorities claimed to know better than the parishioners did.

Isn't this the challenge with everything? How often do we follow like sheep and not take the next step to move deeply to the place within ourselves of KNOWING before we act? How often do we look outside ourselves for the answer and stop there? No one can do it for us. The world will always offer a perspective on everything. It is my job to choose which perspective I will move with in my life, and I want to do it from a place of KNOWING whenever I can get there. I can join with many others who share something with me, but it is up to me to be true to myself and create the meaning that will move me forward. There are lots of examples of belief "moving mountains" because people tapped into this deeper, relentless KNOWING.

In the early 1900s my mother saw the "moving of the mountain" of Mount Rushmore as the presidents' faces were carved into it and the cultivation of an uninhabited land in the plains of South Dakota. After the Civil War, her parents went west from Tennessee. Her family was Baptist and had strong faith that they would be guided and cared for despite life-threatening conditions. As I reflect on what I have seen in my life, there are even greater mountains that have been moved. I have seen the mountain of oppression and fear moved to bring down the Berlin Wall and transform the Soviet Union into free countries. Then, of course, there was Nelson Mandela, who was released from prison after receiving a life sentence and serving twenty-seven years of incarceration. He became the first South African to be elected president in a democratic election, starting his people on a journey to achieve reconciliation. The United States has a first African American president, Barack Obama, whose election amazed and inspired me and millions of others around the world. Women and minorities everywhere are slowly moving through the glass ceiling that had kept them out of the highest positions in government, business corporations, and religion. Now social networking has even been used to successfully overthrow the oppressive government of Egypt. Many mountains are moving. Mountains move slowly and sometimes, in our impatience, we lose sight of our progress.

The Dalai Lama said that he expects to see the major cultural changes in the world come from the women in the Western countries who have education, a mentality for change, a resonance with spiritual guidance and growth, and economic influence in the world. Many mountains have already moved in my lifetime, and I expect to see many more moved.

Learning to Read Intuition

When making big decisions for myself, or listening for the signs that a client is ready for change, I often consider intuitive information: the early signs that point in the direction of the next step before the rational facts come forth. But what is intuition? Most think of it as a means of acquiring awareness without logic or reason. It is information located in the inner world of your experience, which you can find when you look within, read the thoughts and sensations that emerge, and then contemplate and construct their meaning. **Intuitive information powerfully influences beliefs—that "felt inner KNOWING"—which are the outcome of the meaning you have created from your life experience.**

Generally, intuition is understood to be a right hemisphere function that must then be deciphered and put into spoken language by the left hemisphere. Intuition is just another language the brain can learn to read. It is a source of information that requires confidence and trust in the guidance of the inner world. Intuition is often pointed to in the stories of great scientific discoveries and is a primary skill of mystics, prophets, poets, saints, and healers. Intuition is an irrational function in the brain that takes many forms of sensory perception.

We are beginning to develop an understanding about how intuition manifests in the brain and a perspective on the different sensory modalities that can offer intuitive information. We all have different brain styles, and intuition has a style too. Some people tell us they are clairaudient. That means that their auditory system perceives sounds that others do not hear. In personal communications, I have been told of people hearing information in spoken language in their mind about events that are going on around them at the time or a topic that they are contemplating within. In the case of clairaudience, people hear information coming from within and are guided by it.

Another sensory modality for intuition is clairvoyance. Here people report seeing a visual image that is not physically in front of them. It is an image that comes to mind in response to their circumstance, thoughts, or emotions, and is a source of information they must learn to read and interpret. Although people have been labeled as crazy for reporting such experiences, there are lots of intuitives using these skills in the military and in police work. It is also known as remote viewing and extrasensory perception (ESP). For a discussion of this research, see *The Synchronized Universe* by Claude Swanson.[7]

Finally, there is a source of intuitive information that you can read with the Brain-Body Compass by paying attention to the sensations in your body. This is another language to learn to read called clairsentience. The sensations in your body—like goose bumps, chills down your spine, or hair standing up on your neck—are all clairsentient information to decipher.

I do not personally see or hear clairvoyant or clairaudient information as guidance. I do feel a lot of sensations, which is why I developed the concept of the Brain-Body Compass. This is one of my guides to KNOWING. When the needle of my compass is moving and getting my attention with chills down my spine, I stop and consider what is going on and what that sensation is telling me. These are moments when people report inspired insights, which often come without much reflection or reasoning. These aha moments appear to be a source of creativity, wisdom, insights, associations, ideas, applications, solutions, and possibilities. Some people call these "a gift of Grace."

This is the richness of the felt sense identified in the method of Focusing (discussed in chapter 3). The method of Focusing teaches you to read the information registering on your Brain-Body Compass and works with it to access the information and achieve the felt shift you desire. This information source does not have the logical, sequential facts of the left hemisphere. These are bodily sensations and emotions now thought to enter consciousness in the right hemisphere. As Jill Bolte Taylor described, the right hemisphere focuses on the present moment and the whole of what is happening—not the details. These are felt concepts and beliefs that must be interpreted and spoken by the left hemisphere, where language resides. If you think about it, it is not unusual to notice that something is amiss with someone you know well. You feel the change in them or in a group, but your brain doesn't quite know what has changed. You know something is different, but in order to know how to proceed, the left hemisphere has to use language to either inquire or consider how to interpret the new felt sense.

Learning to read the Brain-Body Compass has to do with paying attention to types of sensations, their level and quality of intensity, emotions related to them, the context in which they happen, and the thoughts they trigger. Sometimes they are like a bolt of lightning and sometimes they are as soft as a feather tickling your nose. They create a gut feeling that says yes or no. My awareness of physical intuition, along with an awareness of synchronistic events, has long been a trusted guiding light in my life. I grew up with the concept of Grace being available to me and active in my life.

My mind is often boggled by the experience when it first happens but is then engaged to follow the thread of events that allow my left hemisphere to be able to make sense of the sensations and events. The feeling is hard to describe, but it is always the same inspired pull in a certain direction. When have you been aware of this experience in your own life? Take the time to consider when you have noticed this, how you felt, and how you comprehended the meaning of the feeling. As the next section illustrates, some of my patients have likewise felt intuition and the sensations it activates in us.

Weaving Expanded Awareness into My Clinical Practice

A lot of highly sensitive, intuitive children and adults land in hypoarousal and are exhausted on a regular basis. At least that is what I see in those who come to my office. Many have had care in the mental health system, but it hasn't really helped. Life can be exhausting for them. Because they are receptive to so much information that most people are not, they have to read volumes more inner information than most of us. Drugs to stabilize the nervous system help a little, but aren't really the answer. Learning to read the Brain-Body Compass and the languages of emotion, sensation, intuition, and synchronicity usually changes everything. Here is a story that exemplifies the application of these concepts in clinical practice.

As I became more and more aware of intuitive information and synchronistic events, and as I heard reports from people who have seen changes in their cognitive perceptions of reality as a result, I began wondering about where this information fits in a neuropsychological evaluation of brain function. Parents bring children into the office to better understand and assist them, and they say things like "She is smart and skilled but not working up to her potential," "She seems to be a dreamy kid—off in the clouds, not really with us all the time," and "She likes to spend more time alone than the other kids and seems to tire easily, getting cranky and resistant if she doesn't have her alone time." Parents often also report concern from the teachers that their child may have ADHD, a disorder of attention.

One example of such a situation was Nancy. Her parents were divorced and she was living at a boarding high school. Her parents were concerned that her grades did not reflect her ability and worried that their differences had negatively affected her development. Dad traveled internationally for work and was not always available, even by phone. Mom had remarried and was living in a new community with a new husband and stepchildren. Nancy wasn't happy living with either of them and had settled into boarding school but was described by the teachers as "a dreamy kid who is not always mentally with them during class."

Nancy didn't have much insight into what was going on with her, but she told us she wanted to do well. It was just hard to stay engaged in the academic tasks sometimes. She had figured out that she could focus really well late at night when she got away from everyone and they were all asleep. Then she could stay with the reading, notes, and writing. Her studying was easier and faster. This sounded a lot like her attention was less distracted when alone, so we went with the hypothesis of checking out a possible attentional disorder.

As Nancy did the tasks in the evaluation, it became clear that she was able to focus quite well and able to integrate complex information using her executive functions. The findings in the evaluation seemed to rule out an attentional disorder. As Nancy and I talked, it occurred to me to ask her about the difference in how she felt during the day and at night. She casually mentioned that there was always so much going on when the other students were around all the time. Their presence gave her ideas she found herself thinking about. This prompted me to ask her if she ever had premonitions or KNEW that things were going to happen before they did. She seemed to think that was quite a normal question and said yes. Once there was a prank that was being planned on campus, but no one knew when it was going to happen, until one day she just KNEW it would be that day—and it was. Unfortunately, that awareness grabbed her attention, and her day was spent looking for the prank to happen. With a little exploring, she shared that that kind of awareness was often popping into her mind, except at night when everyone was asleep and she was alone. Nancy didn't hear words in her head or see things in her mind; she felt when things were about to happen and KNEW what they were. She said, "I just go to that place in my head and I KNOW."

When it came time to discuss the results of the testing, Nancy's parents had very different reactions. Nancy's mom was happy to hear about her talents but could not connect with Nancy's intuitive ability. She wanted to know if medication could help tune out these thoughts and distractions during the day. We advised that we would start by helping Nancy recognize what was happening and be more in control of her focus by selecting among and moving through the information she had.

Nancy's dad had a very different reaction. His comment was "Oh, Nancy's just like Grandma. She KNOWS things." Dad's grandmother was well-known as an intuitive in the family, but this had never been shared with Nancy. Dad resolved then and there to spend more time with his daughter, take her on vacation, and tell her about her great-grandmother. He saw them as a lot alike. With this new awareness, Nancy and her parents were better able to understand how her intuition affected her focus and attention and could value and honor her intuitive gifts and help her learn to adjust and use her gifts as an asset. The goal is to learn to observe your experience and make choices for your focus.

They say that everyone has the ability to access intuitive information if they want to. Some listen for it, some develop it in meditation, and some follow it and enjoy the revelations. Some of us are aware of it and others are not. Some of us want to talk about it and learn more. I'm with them. The next section tells a story of intuition, KNOWING, and synchronicity that came to me like three bolts of lightning in one day.

The Gifts of Listening to Intuition

When you're listening to your intuition, things start to flow. On a vacation a few years ago, I was enjoying listening to a CD set on spiritual alchemy by Luanne Oakes, which I had hoped would guide me out of some of the physical aches and pains that had been popping up. As I listened, a brief reference to a book series, *Life and Teaching of the Masters of the Far East*, grabbed my interest and lit up the curiosity that I always listen to.[8] I placed an order for the book to be delivered when I got back and looked forward to reading it on my return.

When the series arrived, I followed my guiding impulse and began reading volume two, having no idea of the journey that was beginning. Slowly, I entered the events of an expedition to India back in the 1890s. It was a story of a group of Americans who had traveled there to learn the ancient wisdom and returned with these tales to tell. At first I did not realize the depth of what was being said, but it gradually became apparent that these researchers, pilgrims, and evolving souls had returned with knowledge of the mysteries of the inner world. When it came to the discussion of their discoveries of oral tradition and written records of St. John the Baptist and Jesus's young life in India, I was totally intrigued. I didn't know they had been in India.

There had been little time to read upon my return from vacation, so by Friday I had not yet finished volume two. But I was eagerly looking forward to the weekend, which held the promise of time to enjoy the story. Upon leaving the office at the end of my day, I paused to chat about this fascinating story with our receptionist, whose father came to this country from India. As I described the story thus far, my enthusiasm increased with the telling and I heard myself say, "Oh, this is so interesting, I want to go to India." Goose bumps came up on my arms at the thought of being there.

Now, that was a most unusual thing for me to say, since I had never before experienced a desire to go to India, and I found all those gods quite confusing. Nonetheless, the words came out of my mouth as I resonated with a sense of young Jesus opening to his Christ Consciousness in India. With that as my parting statement, I left the office and was driving north when the thought came to mind to call a new friend I had met at a conference earlier that year. (This was before the laws prohibiting cell phone use while driving.) She answered the phone immediately and, on inquiring about how she was, she quickly said that she was trying to get a flight to India to go on a retreat there—and would I like to come?

At first I was a bit stunned by the synchronicity of my last spoken statement in the office and this conversation. Chills went down my spine as I heard her words. She went on to tell me about the Oneness University and friends who had attended the twenty-one-day silent retreat. She encouraged me to go online to read about the retreat and see the pictures of the university campus, and she offered to wait on finalizing her flights until I had decided.

Well, this was quite unusual, and my poor brain did not know what to do with it. When something so synchronistic happens, I usually stop in my tracks, listen, and quickly follow. But I had just returned from a vacation and I had a full clinical schedule and two teaching schedules. My left hemisphere said that this was impossible. Having no idea what to do, I did nothing, and instead met another friend for dinner.

The impossibility of the idea of a retreat in India had firmly settled in by the time I arrived home that night, so I felt no rush to go online for more information. Instead, I stood in the kitchen opening the mail. There in the pile was a letter from the bank where my mother had worked for more than thirty years. On opening the letter and reading down the page, shivers again shot through my spine. The bank was writing to inform me that there was a joint account, in my name and my mother's, who had died four years prior, and it contained the exact amount of money for the airfare and retreat in India. And it just happened to arrive that day! Chills ran down my spine again, a sense of importance got my attention, and immediately I KNEW I was going to India, though I had no idea what this was or why I was going. This is the synchronistic type of experience that has always guided me. This was the intuitive felt sense of guidance that was available to me. Such meaningful synchronistic events and the accompanying sensations have long been effective guidance in my life. The belief that it will continue to inform me influences my decisions, whether my left hemisphere can explain it or not.

Obviously, I went to India for the month-long retreat. On the plane ride there, I read the book *Awakening into Oneness* by Arjuna Ardagh, about the Oneness Blessing, or Deeksha.[9] The book talks about a twelve-year-old boy who, in 1988, saw a golden ball of light enter him and was able to pass this Grace of Oneness to the other children in the school. Since then, these beautiful young people have grown in Grace and age and are conducting retreats, including the one I was headed to, for the purpose of opening minds to oneness and conveying Grace all over the world.

By following my North Star to India, I was given a great gift: the ability to further release my mind and move more deeply into feeling, recognizing, and enjoying the subtle energies. Such intuitive and synchronistic experiences are available to everyone if they want to pay attention to that type of information and see where it takes them. These are very subtle distinctions in our experience, and we must learn to recognize them. We live in an exciting time when we are beginning to put into words experiences that were thought to be limited to the saints and sages. Spiritual traditions have more language for this domain than psychology or neuropsychology do right now. Having a background in both, I am attempting to articulate these powerful abilities that are available to us, and I encourage you to consider the times when such coincidental events have turned out to be a significant influence for you. Was there a time when you had shivers down your spine and you paid greater attention because you KNEW something important was happening?

The Trappist monk, mystic, and author Thomas Merton addressed defining intuitive information. He talked about relating in a spiritual reality with aesthetic intuition. After getting out of logic and opening to inspiration by asking and expecting it, the brain is primed to find it. Although the language of the mystics often took on metaphors and concepts of the culture of their times, which may not be as meaningful today, they provided the brain with inspired concepts and images to relate to, activating the sense of being uplifted, and connected to something greater than one's normal perception. But as soon as we come out of our right hemisphere of ineffable awareness, the left hemisphere reaches for something linear and concrete to focus on, trying to nail down the experience in words.

There are no words for the experience of blissful oneness; it is beyond the left hemisphere but available to the Brain-Body Compass. Some of the ancient terms like "Grace" are hard to define from our scientific perspective. But it is under these conditions that I sense that we are beginning to grasp what it is to use our whole brain and access our true potential.

Awakening Applications

◆ Read your body sensations. Watch the videos of Jill Bolte Taylor, Mother Teresa, and Father Bede Griffiths. How do you feel when you hear them speak from the meaning they have created? What is your Brain-Body Compass telling you as you hear their experiences? If you feel a yes in your body, telling you that the meaning they have created is possible for you too, let their example be a light on your own path to meaning.

◆ Create a place to come home to. Adversity will always be a fact of life, but you can weather it by creating a state within yourself to which you return every day. Having something to call on within yourself is a neurochoice you can make. Some people foster this inner strength through meditation, journaling, or— like Mother Teresa—by "praying first." I have found that those who best handle adversity are those who have belief to call on and who have created meaning in their lives.

◆ Read your symbols of meaning. We are often drawn to images or items without consciously knowing why. Look around at the images and objects that hold meaning for you. Reflect on them, and often their meaning will emerge. Let that meaning be a reminder to you of the path you wish to follow.

◆ Read your intuition. Some people receive inner wisdom through clairaudience, clairvoyance, or body sensations. How do you best become aware of your intuition? The next time you have a sense of inner knowing, ask yourself how that guidance came to you so that you can pay special attention to those senses in the future.

♦ Read into synchronicity. When events happen that seem more than just coincidence, ask yourself if they are lining up in such a way that they have special significance. Could it be an invitation to dig deeply within yourself? See where the journey takes you.

Notes

1. Thérèse of Lisieux, *Story of a Soul: The Autobiography of St. Thérèse of Lisieux*, trans. John Clarke, O.C.D. (Washington, DC: Institute of Carmelite Studies, 1972), 207.

2. Philip Booth, "Heading Out," *Selves* (New York: Penguin, 1991).

3. Carol Christ, *Diving Deep and Surfacing* (Boston: Beacon, 1995).

4. Burton Watson, trans., *The Vimalakirti Sutra* (New York: Columbia University Press, 2000).

5. Adapted from Allan Schore, "Right Brain Affect Regulation," *The Healing Power of Emotion*, ed. D. Fosha, J. Siegel, M. Solomon (New York: Norton, 2009), 125.

6. J. Martin, *Between Heaven and Mirth* (New York: HarperCollins, 2011), 15.

7. Claude Swanson, *The Synchronized Universe* (Tucson, AZ: Poseidia, 2003).

8. Baird Spalding, *Life and Teaching of the Masters of the Far East* (Camarillo, CA: DeVorss, 1986).

9. Arjuna Ardagh, *Awakening into Oneness* (Louisville, CO: Sounds True, 2007).

10

Managing Your Awakening Brain: Inner Bridges for Shifting Your State

Wen you are awake to the power of your neurochoices, life is very different. When you develop your skills for reading your Brain-Body Compass and you can decode your emotional information automatically rather than laboriously, you have an awareness of where you are coming from. But what about getting to where you want to go? Reading about all these skills and abilities is a little like studying all the different parts of your car. It's good to know your car so you can keep it functioning effectively and recognize signs of change, but knowing this doesn't put you on the road with an identified destination and method for getting you there.

When you are awake to how this works, you will often see signposts that will expand your ease with the inner world. As David Foster Wallace noted at a 2005 commencement speech at Kenyon College, true freedom "means being conscious and aware enough to choose what you pay attention to and to choose how you construct meaning from experience. Because if you cannot exercise this kind of choice in adult life, you will be totally hosed."[1] As I reflect on what I have learned about using this type of awareness to exchange the state you are in for the one you want to be in, there are three sturdy bridges that can be helpful as you start putting this information to work in your life. In moments of discontent, we all want to be able to recognize the bridge we want, know where to find it, and move across the impasse we face.

The first step is what I call the Freedom Bridge, which leads you out of the unwanted state of reactivity, tension, anxiety, anger, or fear. The second step is the Joy Bridge, which takes you to understanding and possibility. Joy is the ultimate state for your destination on a journey that may start with just achieving some peace, hope, and interest for crafting a desired vision. The third step is traveling the Expansion Bridge, where you take action to create the future you want. This is where your desire actually unfolds. Let's take a look at each bridge and some of the methods for getting yourself across them.

Freedom Bridge: How to Get Immediate Relief from an Unwanted State

When you consider how to get across the Freedom Bridge to relief from the state of negativity you are in, know that the intention is to just release the present resistance to your own satisfaction and joy and be free of the discontent. At first, this is an inside job. It may be as simple as going for a run, a swim, or a game of tennis. Some form of physical exercise can release the physical tension and your body's resistance to ease and harmony. Remember, this is why Dr. Jay teaches isometric exercises in stress management. Releasing the physical tension is a powerful starting point.

Second, consider the thoughts you are thinking. By having power over your thoughts, you have a great influence over your emotions. It is also the doorway to accessing your own constructed meaning and spiritual awareness. When you take charge of your focus, you can choose where you want to go. Although I had understood this intellectually, it wasn't until I was lying on the acupuncture table, feeling my body respond to my thoughts, and watching my thoughts while I was on retreat in India, that I really caught on to the automaticity. Let me explain:

At the Oneness University retreat in India, we meditated a lot. This was familiar to me, given my past spiritual path, but the way they used meditation and their thinking about the mind, as they called it, were different. There were daily workshops to discuss the perspective of the mind they were teaching and group meditations to apply the experiences discussed. They know things about the inner world in India; the traditions are ancient and powerful.

Twenty-one days of intense inner focus can't be summarized, but one of the pearls that came out of the experience for me was the awareness of my own power to release myself from the chatter of my mind. We all perceive the world from our own perspective, and one of mine has to do with considering whether information that comes to me is consistent with what I know about the brain. When they talked about watching the mind, the characteristics and experiences they described were what I would call the brain chatter of the left hemisphere. It was just as Jill Bolte Taylor described it. It was just as I have experienced and seen in my patients.

At the retreat they used somewhat different words to describe what I have been trained to understand as neuropsychological functions. They talked about the emotions that are troublesome as "charges." Having a charge on a particular issue means having reactive emotions in relation to the thoughts of the event. The different emotions of joy, fear, love, disappointment, excitement, and anger all come and go; the retreat leaders talked about these emotions as different personalities rising and ceasing. That makes sense to me from my neuropsychological perspective, although it is not my definition of personality. We do seem like different people in these different emotional states, and they do come and go.

The focus in the retreat workshops was to establish some of the assumptions that govern the mind, which includes your reactions, judgments, and thoughts. Being able to focus on an awareness of those assumptions takes you out of the experience of the thoughts and emotions. Observing my own reaction to something causes me to take it less seriously, believe it less, think about it, and question it more. I get to see what I am doing and choose whether this is an experience I want to continue, rather than believing that the experience is who I am. Repeatedly, I sat in meditation just watching my mind—just watching what was going on in there, not believing it or questioning it. When you can observe the thoughts, you begin to see the assumptions under which you operate. The brain is wired with neural networks that you have trained over the years. If a group were to observe the same event, the meaning might be quite different to each person. It all depends on the neural network you use to view and interpret your experience.

The examples given in the workshops were often quite simple. The workshop leaders were very young Indian monks, both men and women. With open wide eyes and sweet smiles, they had an innocence about them. Emotions, they said, are like a change of clothes. Your essential self is the same at all times, but you put on different clothes for different circumstances. These different clothes are like the different personalities we don with different moods and roles in life. They come and they go, but you—your essential self—stays the same. This is what we watched in meditation. Thoughts, emotions, and assumptions came and went, replaced by new ones.

As I watched my own mind and the thoughts that came and went, I could see the assumptions I had about what was right and wrong; what I was responsible for and must do; what I knew would work out on its own without me; and what piqued my curiosity and pulled me into a stream of associations. It's fascinating to watch what is going on within and experience the whole range of emotions that pop in with the thoughts. It's even better to begin to realize that you don't have to believe it or engage in it. There is a way to learn to just let it go, interrupt yourself mid-sentence, and turn it off.

This type of meditation is a workout to strengthen the executive operating officer, the cingulate. The part of your brain that chooses and sustains your focus is the source of your power to engage or disengage in thoughts, emotions, or activities. The cingulate is a muscle you can strengthen, and it offers you an option for managing your inner world, if you want to. It will get you across the Freedom Bridge, released from the repetitive thoughts, emotions, and sensations that may be holding you back.

This is what I mean when I talk about having a desire to release a resistance. A resistance is a lack of acceptance, a conflict, or a feeling of discontent. The energy of pushing against something fuels it and strengthens it, while dropping resistance opens the bridge to your essential self. The term "resistance" is now being used to identify experiences inconsistent with our essential self as whole and harmonious. Forms of conflict and discontent are considered a resistance to your potential and wellness. Those who teach methods of releasing resistance say all you have to do is learn to let go of the resistance to your own harmony and you find it.

Can it be that simple? Don't all those upsets, fears, and disappointments stay with us somehow and get activated under the next similar circumstances? Lots of psychologists would agree with that. But at the retreat, the monks believed you can sufficiently develop the power of your focus to allow all the unwanted circumstances and your own emotions to just be there. When you do, the "charge" or emotion attached to the thought or event will be released, and you are left with the memory, not the emotion, and the tape in your head stops playing.

The more I watched my thoughts, emotions, states, and "personalities" that arise and observed them from an allowing, accepting, compassionate place within myself, the more they just went away. I didn't engage with the issue, think it through, weigh the pros and cons, get strategic, plan an approach, or discuss it with anyone. I just allowed it to be there, accepting what it was. From that place, the emotion associated with the event just left me.

Call it liberation from the mind or dismantling a neural network. You can have the thought, be aware of an issue, and not be plagued by the emotion. When you refuse to engage with the emotion, you remove the fuel that feeds it. Then a life-altering event is just what it is, not good or bad—just a big experience.

The monks also talked about what it is to reach an awakened state in the spiritual sense. For those that experience awakening, the personalities (emotions) come and go. Emotional feelings move forward in awareness when needed and recede when no longer needed. Emotions are there but not running the show. An expansion in awareness opens this ability to tolerate and allow more in life that previously seemed to be intolerable. This is the ability to observe and recognize but not have to react.

I have a long way to go to understand the neuropsychology of all I experienced at the retreat and in my discovery of the meditation Sat Nam Rasayan, two gifts that came to me through my intention to listen to and follow the messages contained in synchronistic events. I am aware that these experiences are grounded in brain mechanisms and physical complexities that science has yet to fully comprehend. Studying a meditation that guides me through stages of awareness and enables me to release physical sensations of resistance in my body, both in relation to my own thinking and needs as well as in my perception of the suffering of others, is an endeavor I am just beginning. This is the new frontier of how the brain processes the spiritual realm, and although we don't fully understand it, you can certainly try it and benefit from it.

Despite the complexities of the underlying mechanisms, the approach can be remarkably simple: Allowing will take on new meaning for you once you try it. By just letting the unwanted *be*, you disengage your judgments of it. Your resistance to the circumstances determines your emotions. The frustration of wanting it to be different, the anger over injustice, the disappointment over your thwarted expectations—all are yours to hang on to or let go. When you can say, "It is what it is," you release your resistance and pain. Then you are ready to be effective in your action.

Awakening Freedom Applications: What to Do and Where to Look

There are many ways to cross the Freedom Bridge. I have divided them into five different sections to ease your application of these methods. Take the time to consider each of these dimensions of your life, what you are doing now, and what feels to you like a way of growing.

Physical: There are lots of ways to release tension in your body. Isometric exercises can be done anywhere, and other forms of regular exercise, like running, walking, swimming, and dancing, all release tension. There are lots of types of yoga too. Each has a particular focus for increasing strength, regulating energy, and enhancing awareness. The martial arts also offer a way to increase awareness and physical focus. Sports will usually tire you out and release the tensions, and body therapies like massage, acupuncture, reflexology, osteopathy, and acupressure can help to get you back in balance. A regular sleep cycle really helps too. Nutrition and hydration play an important part, along with limiting stimulants like caffeine or depressants like alcohol. Herbs and supplements enhance your nervous system and ease your muscles. These are general suggestions, and if you are interested in getting guidelines specifically tailored to your needs, seeking out a naturopath or a nutritionist would be a good place to start.

Cognitive and Emotional: Meditation is the single most effective method for strengthening control over your thoughts and emotions. There are lots of types of meditation, and if done frequently your brain gets a break from the constant stimulation and is better able to maintain harmony. Mindfulness meditation is very popular and easily accessed. There are audio recordings you can listen to and classes you can attend. Kundalini yoga, the yoga of awareness, and the meditations included in the practice use breath and focus to specifically target the release of tension in the body and the regulation of the autonomic nervous system. Another practice I recommend is Sat Nam Rasayan, the meditation for releasing resistance, which we feel physically. The Buddhist method of Tonglen is a meditation in which you breathe in an awareness of the problem, recognizing the sensations of unwanted reactions, and then breathe out while focusing your thoughts and emotions on compassion for all those involved in the conflict. By pairing your breath with your awareness of the resistance and then adding compassion, you regulate the autonomic nervous system and shift your thoughts and emotions. Again, these recommendations may not all be for you, but they are starting points for you to research and explore until you discover what works for you.

Therapies: There are lots of therapies designed to release stress. The key is being aware of the physical sensations, thoughts, and emotions, and learning to let go of them. Self-hypnosis is a method that induces a hypnotic state through self-suggestion. Hypnotherapy is a method for moving your awareness from one mental state to another in response to a hypnotic suggestion by the hypnotherapist. Once experienced, people readily recognize the inner path for using self-hypnosis or self-suggestion in their thoughts to shift from an unwanted state to a desired state. Somatic Release is a therapy in which a trained therapist guides you to allow an awareness of the physical and emotional feelings and, by doing so, release them. The therapist guides your focus to releasing the sensations, instead of telling the story of the trauma the sensations represent. The HeartMath Freeze-Frame method has been widely studied and is a way of putting your brain on pause when you are experiencing the resistance of hyperarousal.

It is easily used in a business or personal interaction and has been shown to improve physical and mental health. Thought Stopping and the Stop and Think Approach are examples of therapies in psychology for taking greater control of your thoughts and the emotions that come with them. To find these resources, please see my website, awakeningthebrain.com, to start researching services in your area.

Recreation: We use the word *recreation* for our hobbies and play time because they re-create and restore us. Some hobbies will engage your brain and body in a harmonious way that is designed to decrease activity in the language centers that play the negative self-talk tapes in your head. Here you can give the language centers a rest by activating the visual processing system with physical activity. Gardening, caring for animals, sculpting, painting, knitting, sewing, decorating, hiking, kayaking, skiing, and bird-watching are just a few that can re-create and restore you.

Spiritual Practice: Almost all these methods can be part of a spiritual practice if you bring the spiritual meaning to the experience. Prayer, mantras, the rosary, chanting, meditation, ritual, music, singing, dancing, walking, or eating meditation—these are just a few of the spiritual practices that can restore you to harmony. They all have long histories and religious or cultural meaning, which is very powerful for stabilizing your internal world.

Since I have used all the methods mentioned here, I can highly recommend them. Once you find what works for you and become disciplined in practicing it, you will find it easier to shift your emotions when they hijack you. If you want to get to the other side of the Freedom Bridge, try any or all these suggestions and find the ones that are right for you today. Be open to the ones that will be right for you tomorrow.

Joy Bridge to Understanding and Envisioning Possibilities

The sign that points you toward the second step, the Joy Bridge, is like the road sign that points you in the direction of the city at the end of your destination. Here we are talking about achieving a conscious understanding of the unwanted experience you are having, the events that got you there, and what you can do about them. From here you can figure out what will take you to the desired destination. Once you are over the Freedom Bridge and no longer trapped in negativity and out of the unwanted state you were in, the Joy Bridge is for getting into the state you want and deciding where you are going before you take off.

Understanding the problem, how it got that way, and how it all works is usually the starting point for resolving most challenges in life. However, the field of mental health has generally not focused on the health side and looks instead at pathology or what's wrong. Although this is starting to change with the advent of new thinking like Positive Psychology, we know more about our pathology than the means of getting out of it and accessing our potential.

When you have gotten over the Freedom Bridge and are ready to reflect on the challenge from a more peaceful place within you, in the Optimal Arousal Zone where your creativity resides, approach it from a more general perspective first. Don't dive back into the same thorny details that reactivate the same emotions and produce the same perspective that reinforces the state you are moving out of. Consider how you have seen such things resolved in the past, the kinds of positive outcomes you are drawn to, and whom you respect in such circumstances. Step back and see where the big picture of the unwanted experience and circumstances are pointing. Get perspective on what you do want and how it would feel to have what you want, which is usually the opposite of the current circumstance.

Attempt to ground yourself in an expectation that there are answers to questions and solutions to every problem. Move into your Expect and Detect focus. Rather than looking for who is to blame, ask questions about what can be done. What exactly is your goal? What would be the first step in an action plan aimed at the outcome you desire? Check how each step of the way feels. Determine whether it is progress in the right direction or more of the reactivity.

When you take this approach, you regulate your limbic system to balance your emotions each step of the way, which enhances your creativity for problem solving. Now you are using all those fibers that come down from the cortex for awareness to listen to and guide your limbic system of emotions. This is stepping back to a perspective that is broader, engaging your right hemisphere where you can see the whole of the issues. Here the glitches are less emotional and more easily observed. Both of these keep you more in touch with your gut sense, which is sensitive to the feeling of the outcome you desire. Focus on your Brain-Body Compass to recognize the possibilities you seek. When you regulate your state, you have greater access to the resources of your whole brain.

Another way to move forward from an unwanted state or circumstance is to dismantle the old neural network in your brain that either created the problem in the first place or is preventing you from recognizing the way out. Einstein said that a problem cannot be solved using the same thinking that created it. The trick is all about getting out of the old thinking and getting into a more creative and effective perspective. When the old thinking is deconstructed—by not returning there and not giving it any more reinforcement—there is room for a new vision, and when the new path that thinking provides is built with continued practice, it becomes automatic.

A good grasp of the complexity of the problem changes how you think, what you expect, and what you do. However, it doesn't always achieve the feeling state you desire. You can understand it and still not like it. You can have insight and cope and still be in pain. But understanding gives you a new way to reason about the problem. It is the beginning of changing the thinking that created the problem in the first place. In some ways it changes how you feel because it helps you not feel lost and confused and reactive. When you get out of those emotions, you have access to more of your cognitive skills for problem solving. When you feel afraid, all you can see is the threat and all you can feel is the cascade of chemical reactions that happen within your brain. When you feel confident and curious, your brain starts zeroing in on the possibilities that you can make happen. This is the neurochoice you have available to you to change your brain's chemistry and access your talent.

When I took the EST seminar many years ago, they talked about how understanding your state didn't help you achieve the personal growth you were seeking. In those days there were lots of folks that had done psychoanalysis and psychotherapy and had gotten more entrenched in their story. They did not feel better.

Understanding can be achieved without resulting in real change. In fact, retelling the story over and over strengthens the neural network that contains the unwanted state. Stepping back from the story and dismantling the dysfunctional neural network requires that you replace it with a new perspective from which you can achieve a new experience. You can act more effectively if you let go of trying to control the uncontrollable, find a place of hope and possibility within, and reach for less judgment and more acceptance. Understanding won't necessarily take you over the Joy Bridge, but it can give you the information to get you to it.

Awakening Joy Applications: What to Do and Where to Look

Physical: All the ways for keeping your body in a state of harmony to get across the Joy Bridge are the same as getting across the Freedom Bridge. You will be more effective in recognizing why things are happening, what you would rather do, and how to achieve your vision if you consistently and deliberately release the tensions in your body; this way, you can access the information that is there for you to better understand your situation and wisely construct your vision. Keep exercising, eating, hydrating, and sleeping, and you will be more effective.

Cognitive and Emotional: As you explore an understanding of your challenge and build a vision of your desire, be aware of the physical sensations in your body and the guidance of your Brain-Body Compass. This is your constant guide to KNOWING more precisely what could work for you as you consider possible insights and actions. By deliberately interpreting the information from your experience, you can first form a conscious vision of the solution and then use the physical sensations to assess its accuracy as well as to guide you in its execution. Your emotions and thoughts are constantly changing and require regular interpretation. This is a gift that really good therapists, supervisors, teachers, parents, and leaders have perfected. To stay focused on the target, keep reading the situation and adapting your vision.

Therapies: There are lots of therapeutic methods that can assist you in the process of gaining insight and understanding and developing a new perspective. There is psychoanalysis and lots of different types of psychotherapy. Some therapies are done individually; some are available in groups. Therapies include insight-oriented, expressive, family, interpersonal, narrative, integrative, body-oriented, and brain-oriented. The list goes on and on. There are lots of types of therapy because there are lots of types of problems. Find a therapist who is knowledgeable about your challenge and is on your wavelength. Just pay attention to how you feel, and don't get stuck focusing on the problem instead of the solution. Listen to the Brain-Body Compass to regulate your emotional balance. That alone will keep you smarter and more effective.

Recreation: When you are in the thick of sorting out a thorny problem, don't drop the activities and interests that keep you stable. The same hobbies that can assist you in getting across the Freedom Bridge will continue to stabilize you while you sort out an understanding of the unwanted experience you face and access your skills to address it. Hobbies bring harmony, happiness, and satisfaction; that is why we do them. Keep doing the activities that stabilize you when you are faced with a challenge. These are the times of distraction from the problem, which enable your brain to consolidate what you have learned and bring forth new insights for solutions.

Spiritual Practices: There are spiritual practices like discernment that allow you access to greater awareness and insight. Each religion and spiritual orientation has practices like prayer that orient your focus to reaching beyond yourself to the experience of belonging to something greater that you can call on to guide you. When you reach that spiritual state within, you have access to more insight and awareness of the possibility for understanding what is going on and the directions for change.

Expansion Bridge to Create the Future: Taking the Action That Will Produce Your Vision

Finally arriving at the Expansion Bridge means you have moved out of the unwanted state you were in and shifted in your emotions and are ready for a new direction, which will promote your growth. On the Expansion Bridge, you are taking action from a place in yourself where success is assured. Here you must keep observing the information from your Brain-Body Compass as you travel because it is new territory. Following your compass means correcting your direction as you go and learning to deal with all the different emotions you encounter, wanted and unwanted.

There are times when it works well to use the intense emotion of an unwanted situation to be the fuel for sustaining your effort to achieve a better outcome. However, it usually works out better when you have first envisioned an outcome that feels right and then stay focused on it. There are examples of this in the little and big things in life. In either case, keeping an eye on what you want—your intention for your actions—will help you transform all that frustration, powerlessness, and irritability into the energy to move forward. You can turn frustration into fuel.

One of my earliest memories of discovering this within myself happened when I was a young child. I was maybe seven or eight years old, and I used to play with a neighbor down the street. Lucy and I were the same age, went to the same school, and lived on the same block. We often would be outside with lots of open fields to explore. Lucy had a younger brother, Jerry, who loved to torment her, and when we were together, I was not spared. Jerry took particular delight in sneaking up on us to startle us with the garter snakes that were so prevalent in the area. When he found one, he caught it by the neck close to the head, snuck up behind us, and shoved it in our faces. Of course, to his delight, we would jump, scream, and run from such a startling experience. Jerry thought this was funny, but I didn't.

Over time, the repetition of this startling and upsetting experience got me thinking. I didn't like being scared. I didn't like scary movies or amusement park thrills. This wasn't fun to me. I didn't know anything about the fight-or-flight response or the autonomic nervous system—I just didn't like being scared. After a while it finally dawned on me that if Jerry, who was younger than I was, could pick up the snake, I could too. That was a revelation. It was only a thought, but it was a thought that made me feel better. I liked to lie in the grass and watch the clouds go by, looking for the shapes and faces that they contained. Being afraid of the snakes was messing that up too.

Finally, one day the frustration of Jerry and the garter snakes just became intolerable, and I decided to see if I could find a snake and pick it up myself. They weren't hard to find and they weren't all that fast either. In fact it was kind of easy to catch one, and suddenly there I was with a snake in my hand. Just like that, all the tension and fear was gone. I could do this. But what about Jerry? What did I have to do to get him to stop?

After brief reflection, I decided to give Jerry a little of his own medicine. With snake in hand, I found where he was playing and came charging along just as he had done to me. Jerry didn't like it either. He jumped just like I had and began to run. Well, that was all I needed to see. I will never forget chasing Jerry all the way down the block and watching him disappear into the door of his house. I stood there on the sidewalk, taking in what had just happened, and I realized that neither Jerry nor the snakes had any power over me. I let the snake go then and there and have never picked up another one. I have never needed to. I was free. My unwillingness to tolerate the discomfort and my desire to be rid of the fear had been the fuel I needed to solve that problem.

Each time I tell this story, I still laugh, especially at the image of Jerry running into his house. The moments of victory are sweet and very freeing. They come along all the time in little things and in big things. Paying attention to what you have learned makes a difference.

Yes, the big things seem to operate on the same principles. The basic dynamic that has worked for me with the pain I experienced from my sister's brain injury is pretty similar to the dynamic of Jerry and the snake. I didn't like either, and each time the frustration came up, I resolved to find a way out of it. The problem of Jerry and the snake didn't take that long. I didn't enjoy scaring or hurting him. But I knew I wanted to be rid of the fear and get him to stop.

My experience with Jerry was a little example of envisioning an outcome and staying focused on it. A bigger example was my experience overcoming the pain of my sister's injury, which took decades and shaped my career. The impact of her injury on my family and me was so big that there was no quick fix. With each new struggle in the family, I more deeply resolved to learn something that could help. My career path allowed me to create a meaning and purpose from the unwanted situation we faced; it gave me broader motivation to continue my efforts. In the '80s, I first learned about the neuropsychological effect of airborne toxins, and I began to realize what had happened to my sister. That is also when she had a neuropsychological evaluation and, finally, an interpretation for her emotional and cognitive dysfunction. Slowly over the next decade and into the new millennium, she received the care and support services that have been stabilizing for her. Her journey—and my reactivity to it—has produced substantial knowledge about brain injury and treatment methods for me and those I can share them with.

That's how I turned frustration into fuel, and many, many others have done the same. In fact, changing a sense of powerlessness into action is the energy that created the "New World" in the Americas. People who were in undesirable situations got up and got out and took their chances on their ability to create something better. It's the same energy that took so many people to Australia and other countries where there was opportunity for immigrants. Activism is often the ability to look squarely at what you don't want and then choose to turn in the exact opposite direction and create what you do want. Support groups, fund-raisers for providing a means for services, research providing new alternatives for health, energy, education, transportation—the list goes on and on.

There are lots of ways to promote solutions by using your pain, discomfort, tension, or dissatisfaction to propel you forward.

This was the thrust of Mother Teresa's life. She saw suffering and felt called to act. India needed her compassion and activism. Because she was able to see the need and felt called to do something, millions of people received assistance who would not have otherwise. When people use frustration and discontent as fuel, they are changed—and amazing innovations result.

Awakening Your Future Applications: What to Do and Where to Look

Physical: As you progress over the days, weeks, months, or even years to achieve your goal, take care of your body. Don't let yourself get too tired, hungry, thirsty, or angry. Move often and release tension clearing the body for clearer information to come to your brain. Your frustration can be the fuel to create a strong and healthy body as you release your tensions and overcome obstacles.

Cognitive: Every vision is simply a hypothesis about what you think will work using the information you have right now. Visions have underlying principles that don't change, but the steps for getting there constantly *do* change. When I picked up the snake, I did not envision chasing Jerry down the street and into his house. I just wanted to get him to stop by giving him a dose of his own medicine. When I realized my sister had suffered a toxic encephalopathy, I didn't even know what that was or what it did to the brain. My vision was broad and vague, but I knew I wanted to learn and offer some options to my family. Being aware of what you know and what you don't know enables you to build your knowledge and learn its implications for what you can do. As you go over the Expansion Bridge, you are entering new territory and gaining new insights that should keep developing your vision, making it more specific and effective with each new insight. The cognitive work of analyzing the information you have and determining what you can do is at the heart of a successful journey to the other side of the Expansion Bridge, which moves you from hope to possibility to a new, actualized reality you desire.

Emotional: On the Expansion Bridge, you will experience lots of different emotions. Hope can get you started, and some success can bring you relief. When you form a possibility for achieving your goal, enthusiasm can keep you going. Disappointment can take you backward. Remember Theory U: Don't act until you get to KNOWING. Get past your critical voice of judgment to an open mind and past your cynicism and fear to an open heart. Then your open mind will effectively guide you so that you won't get stuck in your own reactivity and confusion. Listen to your emotions as guidance and use your cognition to interpret the information and envision the solution.

Therapies: My experience of releasing the fear of garter snakes is consistent with methods of behavior modification that use exposure. That means you are assisted in tolerating the presence of the thing that triggers your fear. This is often done for people who are anxious in elevators or airplanes, or when driving over bridges. By having someone teach you how to release your anxiety response and focus your intention, and then support you in sustaining that effort, you can be free of the grip of anxiety. The treatment method of Focusing, which I explained in chapter 3, applies as well. By being aware of the felt sense of an issue and by constantly reevaluating your approach when you are not engaged and are just observing its meaning, it is possible to achieve an understanding of the meaning it has for you. Then you can take meaningful and effective action.

Recreation: Again, hobbies are stabilizing for your inner world when you are on a challenging journey over the Expansion Bridge. They give your body and brain time to step out of the fray and be restored to balance. Don't stop doing the things that restore your resources when you are undertaking the long-distance run to the finish line you have chosen. Keep replenishing your resources, and pace yourself. The turtle won the race over the hare. Keep consistent and you will get there intact.

Spiritual Practices: Regular spiritual practices like meditation or ritual will keep you grounded in a physical state, an emotional balance, a cognitive expectation, and guided action. Creating meaning from a deeper place strengthens your resolve and gives you access to broader and deeper resources within you. Call on that which is greater than yourself and you will get an answer.

There are lots of careers like mine where you can channel your frustration and be a part of creating a better world. All the service professions, like medicine, hospice, psychology, social services, Peace Corps, and environmental ecology, are ways of letting go of reactivity and expressing both frustration with our world and a passion to improve it. Anyone who brings personal meaning to their work is achieving this.

When I read the words from David Foster Wallace, which I quoted earlier in this chapter, I was delighted to see a concise description of the message that has taken me a whole book to explain. But I reflected for days on what it would be like to "be totally hosed." It sounds like what my generation might call being overwhelmed or bombarded. It aptly captures the complexity of our technological age, in which we are being bombarded constantly. As I thought about his words, it seemed to me that the only way you get to really enjoy this life experience is to get some deliberate control of it. Then you can make your attempts, learn from your mistakes, grow from your process, witness your effectiveness, and enjoy your fulfillment.

This is not new news, but we are seeing it in a new way thanks to neuropsychology and neuroscience. Each generation must redefine essential truths of existence and express them in the language of the times. Learning to make neurochoices that enable you to claim your power, act effectively, and enjoy your life requires that you achieve focus and alignment with your intention. Each generation must find its own way to achieve the alignment that will move it forward under its conditions.

We can learn from the masters of the past, follow the established educational, religious, and spiritual traditions, and use knowledge like the concepts offered here. But you must select from the resources to take the next step, and then the step after that, toward the fullness of life you are drawn to. My wish for you is that you take deliberate control of your day and use all the powerful resources available to move regularly into a state of ease first, focus on the bridge that is right for you today, and have a great ride!

Note

1. David Foster Wallace, "David Foster Wallace on Life and Work," *Wall Street Journal*, http://online.wsj.com/article/SB122178211966454607.html (accessed 10/7/2011).

Epilogue

When I planned the chapters for *Awakening the Brain,* my original intent was to explain brain structures and neuropsychological functions like choice of focused attention, holding an intention in working memory, and regulating emotion in conjunction with the power of belief. After explaining these abilities of the brain, my primary goal was to explore the spiritual dimension of the brain we all have. This is a recent area in neuroscience that is identifying the brain changes occurring with spiritual practice by studying the brains of monks, nuns, and those committed to similar practices. This book was supposed to contain three additional chapters: "The Brain and Creating a Spiritual Practice," "An Integrated Mind: Finding Alignment," and "The Neuropsychology of Grace: Alignment with Higher Consciousness." Unfortunately, I discovered it was not possible to put a life's work into one book.

This realization initiated a plan for a second book, *Awakened Brains: Tales of Transcendence*. Now my plan is to write a continuation of the concepts introduced in *Awakening the Brain* but dedicate this next book to exploring spiritual experience in relation to brain function. Since the final chapters have already been written, expanding on these concepts is the logical next step. Taking the findings of neuroscience and neuropsychology and demonstrating them in real-life human experience has been the basis of my success in treating the brains of those who have come to me over the years. Those who have engaged the power of belief have progressed beyond my expectation. How do those with awakened brains perceive the world? How are their emotions, thoughts, and behavior different because of their spiritual experience? These are some of the intriguing questions to be explored in my next book. I look forward to sharing these thoughts with you in the near future.